T0095339

Fail to Yield

by
Mi. Odle

iUniverse, Inc.
Bloomington

Fail to Yield

Copyright © 2011 Mi. Odle

All rights reserved. No part of this book may be used or reproduced by any means, graphic, electronic, or mechanical, including photocopying, recording, taping or by any information storage retrieval system without the written permission of the publisher except in the case of brief quotations embodied in critical articles and reviews.

iUniverse books may be ordered through booksellers or by contacting:

iUniverse
1663 Liberty Drive
Bloomington, IN 47403
www.iuniverse.com
1-800-Authors (1-800-288-4677)

Because of the dynamic nature of the Internet, any Web addresses or links contained in this book may have changed since publication and may no longer be valid. The views expressed in this work are solely those of the author and do not necessarily reflect the views of the publisher, and the publisher hereby disclaims any responsibility for them.

Any people depicted in stock imagery provided by Thinkstock are models, and such images are being used for illustrative purposes only.

Certain stock imagery © Thinkstock.

ISBN: 978-1-4620-6880-7 (sc)
ISBN: 978-1-4620-6881-4 (hc)
ISBN: 978-1-4620-6882-1 (e)

Library of Congress Control Number: 2011961229

Printed in the United States of America

iUniverse rev. date: 11/15/2011

Contents

CHAPTER 1
Beautiful Smile

Sue was lying asleep in the bed; her hands were cold, there were bruises on her arms and hands where needles had been put in, and there were tubes in her nose so she could breathe. She made no movement; she had no expression. The intensity of her spirit was unexplainable.

Sue's husband, Toby, was standing around, deciding who could come and go in her hospital room. He might say he was saddened by her lying there motionless, but his attempt to control the crowd was beyond meaningless.

A nurse came into the room to take Sue to get an MRI. Toby was glad to see that; he said, "There is a pretty nurse coming to see me. Here I am; sit on my lap." He tried to give her a hug, but the nurse refused and looked with disgust at the old pervert.

Another nurse came to help take Sue to the MRI. The two nurses tried to take Sue's bed and turn it around at the same time; Toby was giving them orders on how to turn the bed. Toby followed the nurses and continuously directed them, saying they should do better.

Meanwhile, Sue's younger son, Joe, and his wife, May, with her older son, Dan, and his wife, June, were sharing their thoughts about how their mother was doing; Sue was mother to three children, two sons and an older daughter, along with seven grandchildren (two granddaughters and five grandsons). Sue's illness happened so fast that they did not know how serious it was or what was the matter.

June tried to explain to Joe and May, along with May's son, Otto, that she might live another month, if not another week, or Sue might die any day. As she calmed down, May could not help the tears that fell down her face. One hour passed by. The nurse brought Sue back to her room; Toby came along behind, directing the nurse how to place her in the bed. Sue didn't care; no doubt she would prefer to sleep in, and who could blame her? Otto had to return to work the next day, as did Joe. There were lots of hugs and tears.

As May came close to Sue to hug her, without warning, Sue smiled at her from ear to ear. Her eyes were bright as twinkling stars, and her face was shining; the whole room was luminous. It was essential to organic life, visible in darkness; it was a shining bright light, a moment of hope and love, a last-minute life-and-death, spirited, invigorating smile given to May. This moment touched Otto, whose tears came like a river. Aunt June hugged May and started crying; Joe was in shock. Then May gave Sue a hug and said to her, "I love you, Grandmam."

Grandfather Toby was also crying; he looked like he was having a heart attack, but he was not. With a mocking, cynical cry that was loud enough for every person to hear, he said, "She is smiling; look at her smile!" He was weeping and talking at the same time. Toby could not stop smiling; Joe just stood and looked at May.

"Are you okay?" Joe asked softly, and then May hugged her grandmother. "Do not stop smiling; keep smiling. Everything is going to be okay. I love you." She gave her a hug, hoping to see her again.

Sue smiled for about five seconds, and then she went back to sleep, like nothing had happened. Grandmother smiled to May that day, and then she became at peace for her life. It was impossible to have dry eyes; she cried and cried, feeling sorry that she might not see her again and had not told her grandmother she loved her.

May always wanted to be with her father. But her dad was not there when she needed him. When May was three years old, she came to Korea from Japan with her dad, Mr. Kim. May did not remember or know him; he sent few greetings to her. She married Joe and became pregnant in Korea and came to America; she had two children with Joe. She needed her father's help, but he was not there to help her. She wanted to give up the American life, but she did not give it up. She has been here for thirty-five years. She had to work to save her children; she had to work with her hands or in an office. But she was fired from every job for arguing with coworkers who were not doing their job.

Eventually, her children got married and moved out from under her wing. After her house was empty, she felt shallow and removed the contents after years of neglect. As a result, she had a mild heart attack. She had to do something to improve her physical health. Every stress she had comforted with food, like fried chicken, mashed potatoes, and more. She became overweight. May stopped working and took care of herself. She started walking four to five miles a day, each day. Then an extraordinary thing happened during her morning walk. Her father appeared in her thoughts, smiling to her, and May spoke to him. In her vision, she was visiting while she was in high school, she was wearing her school uniform, and they were on the front porch of his house. She vividly saw him smile that morning. It was so special, and she could not let go of it. She had been looking for her father since she was three years old. Sue's father, Kim, gave her positive affirmation, so she would not stop walking.

When May lost her mother overseas, she no longer had a family. May took her husband Joe's family as her new family. Trying to help this family was not easy, and Joe was not always easy to live with; he often treated her with contempt. But Grandmother Sue did give her peace and forgiveness to the family. It was a hurtful, malicious, and distressed journey. But the feelings of hate, hostility, and mental wounds were deflated with Sue's beautiful smile.

Chapter 2
Back Surgery

In September 2007, Sue was in the hospital with a back problem. Toby was unfaithful, abusive, and vituperative; he believed that he was perfect. Everything had to be his way or the highway. He thought the city was too crowded, so they moved to the country, twenty miles from the city. But in the winter, there was so much snow in the driveway, they could not get out. They did not think about how difficult it was to live in the country in their old age. They had no neighbors; it was a perfect place to control another person's pride.

They did very well the first year. With the little money they had saved, they purchased new furniture and more. They had an open house; Toby bragged that this was a dream home for him. They invited friends and family, and met new friends. After one year, Sue began to have complaints about her husband. One day, they were cleaning the garage; there was an oil spot on the floor. She had to clean and clean, but she could not get the oil spot out of the garage. He pushed and pushed her; she had to bend her knees and make the garage floor spotless. She had to clean the house until it was spotless. Every day, she had to clean, and the house had to be the perfect place; they had to eat at the perfect time and then go to bed. She did this every day, and then one day while she was bending her knees to clean the back porch, she cracked her back. She had pulled her back muscle. She thought the pain would go away in a few days, but it did not. It got worse, and she could not walk with the pain in her back.

She went to see the doctor to get medication for the pain in her back, which was not going away. The doctor decided the best option for her was surgery. After she had the surgery, the pain was gone, but she had a problem with walking. Her feet did not work normally; every step when walking was an extreme struggle, and she could not walk up steps or a little hill. She had to use a walker to get around, and she had to be on a flat surface to walk. She needed help to get out of bed or go to the bathroom. Surgery might have helped the pain in her back, but her back had no feeling when she walked. The steps that she had to take to walk were not connected with her brain. Her brain was not working as it should. On the other hand, she was doing as well as she could, cooking and doing house chores. In her old age, she had to prove that she was loved by her husband, if he was to love her. What would he do if having her as his wife was too much? Afterward, she was not herself. Her physical health began to deteriorate quickly. One day, May and Joe brought her favorite food, pizza. As they were eating, she needed to go to the bathroom; when she was in the bathroom, she needed help and called for her husband. Toby answered, "I am eating; you have to wait!" He screamed like a child that he needed to finish his dinner before he could help her.

That day, May and Joe saw that she was in extreme pain. Toby was abominable and reluctant; he was conscience-stricken that they saw what kind of a person he was. When he finished the food on his plate and went to help her, Joe and May heard her crying but did not know why she was crying, and then he said something to her they could not understand. Maybe his big hands were pulling up her pants too hard, or he was too rough, or she was upset because her husband did not help her into the bathroom.

May and Joe were ashamed; they looked at each other and wondered what they could do to help her get out of her pain—should they ignore it or what? They thought Toby was not going to stop biting until she was no longer dependent on herself. If not, she was going away to stay with her family. Sue pleaded, "My spirits were no longer with him. I came to peace of mind; please, help me."

This should not have happened to Sue; it could have been avoided. But the family did not act responsible for their mother. They might say they dearly loved their mother, but May did not hear it, and their actions on the last day showed she was in pain. May could not explain that it was the truth in reaction to Sue. Many things were showing; they were coldhearted and played the game of life as their own. May only knew one thing: Joe was hurt and sad that she struggled to stay alive. He did not know how to help or what to say. In her mind, that struggle was over; she sat still, and the whole universe slowed down like her motion.

CHAPTER 3
Colon Cancer

After Sue had back surgery, the doctor found she had colon cancer. It was unexpected to the family. The doctor took out a foot-long section of her colon. She became aware of her mortality. Her husband was abusive every day as vengeance. Every time the family visited, he complained regardless of whether she felt good or not. He had to have some issue to talk about. One day May and Joe visited Sue at the hospital; she was doing fair. May cooked homemade noodles with chicken broth. Sue was delighted and had some lunch, and then she saved some for dinner. The meal relaxed her and helped her sleep.

As she was sleeping, Toby asked everyone to let her take a nap and they could go to another room. He knew he was the center of attention. Shortly, he criticized his two sons. One son, Dan, was an airline pilot; the other son, Joe, was a truck driver. Toby started to ridicule and mock Joe for being a truck driver. Toby was sitting with Dan and June, and with Joe and May sitting by; Toby said, "Yesterday, I was driving to see your mom, and this dumb trucker cut in front of me, almost hitting the front of my car! That dumb trucker needed to slow down!"

The brothers looked at each other and their wives, shaking their heads and wondering what to say to each other. Then Toby began to ramble on about Japanese people. Dan and June just sat there looking at May; Joe did not say anything but had a smirk on his face. May could not take it; she had to get out of there and get away from Toby. Joe's brother did not defend him, but what was Joe's smirk about? How could a father choose one son over another? It was humiliating.

Did he feel sorry? Did he take offense? Sue's back problem could have been avoided. Dan could not see yet; he sat proudly with his father, paying attention to Toby and acting spellbound. May did not see Toby feeling sorry for his wife; rather, he was showing attention to his other son. He favored one son over the other, to whom he was barbarous and endlessly abusive. He was their father, or was he? May often asked, but there was no answer; rather than a father, it seemed he was a sexual predator. He thought carrying a big gun made him a big man, but he was no less insecure than a little bug. The saints are sinners who keep trying; they have no mercy and are cruel, inhumane, and stony hearted.

CHAPTER 4
What Happened? Not a Surprise

In August 2007, Sue and Toby decided to move back from the country to be closer to the hospital and doctor's office. Toby began complaining that she was hard to take care of; he said he was overworked because he had to help her; due to that, he was tired. Most of all, he said she did not need that walker to get around. But she had no defense. Sue was confounded, puzzled by what he said; she ignored what he did.

The family looked at each other and asked, "What does it matter?"

May looked at the family, because it did matter. Her walker was her life support; she needed it to get around. May had no choice but to be quiet and sit there, to be a little Asian woman who did not know English.

In October 2008, Sue had to go to the bathroom in the middle of the night due to a kidney infection. She woke up and looked for her walker, but it was not there. She called her husband, asking for the walker. Joe answered with anger, pointing to Sue and saying, "You do not need the walker! I moved the walker over there!"

Trying to help her go to the bathroom, he grabbed her and

dropped her onto the cement floor. He dropped her so hard she screamed, she could not get up or stand by herself. She had to go to the emergency room that night and have another MRI. The MRI showed her lung had been bruised when he had picked her up with his big farmer's hands; it must have been squeezed harder than normal as he was lifting and dropping her onto the floor. Her tailbone was swelling with the bruise and so was her kidney. The next day, the family rushed to the hospital. She lay in the bed with no movement of life. She looked like she had been bitten by some big animal all over her body.

Joe and May walked into the room; Toby was trying to comfort her, saying, "Look who's here to see you."

Joe and May were shocked to see her; they had seen her two weeks earlier, and she had been doing fine then. At this moment, they felt completely lost.

Should they cry or stay unruffled?

The doctor stopped by, and Toby told him that she had fallen while trying to go to the bathroom. Then he told the doctor she had Alzheimer's disease and her kidneys were failing, as well as her lungs and hearing. The doctor looked at him and said, "She is going to be okay. She does not have Alzheimer's disease; she just needs some rest."

After the doctor left, Joe and May were glad to hear the truth. The following week, they stopped by to see how she was doing. She was coming along well, and she was happy to see Joe and May. Then May asked Sue what had happened that day.

She explained that she could not remember that day but said her tailbone area had been bruised and the bruise was black. Did the doctor know? May said yes, the doctor knew, but what could he do? Joe and Dan's sister Lake called, saying Sue was dying with kidney, lung, and heart failure. They had to be there for

Grandmam right now. Dan had to call in for work; he flew from out of state, and Joe drove two hours to be there. They could not believe what they were hearing; the doctor had said that she just needed a little rest, she was going to be fine, and she did not have Alzheimer's disease. The brothers were angry about why their mother was in the hospital with bruises on her body.

What did Lake know that the brothers did not know? The following year, Sue's sister passed away. She became stressed and was not eating as she should. Toby became an abuser and bully. Every day she had to get him clothes to wear, her shoes had to be on her feet. She wanted to lie in the bed, but he made her take a nap in the living room in the recliner for just an hour, and then she had to get up and bake him an apple pie (his favorite dessert).

Again and again, Toby complained about her walker. He was determined that she did not need it. She just got out of the hospital and she just buried her sister not too long ago. Yet Toby wanted to take away her walker. Sometimes, he did not want her to use the walker in public with him, but she had to use the walker to go shopping at the supermarket or to go anyplace with friends.

At the same time, Junk (Lake's son) lived with them, and Cary (Lake's daughter) brought Nick, their great-grandchild, for them to babysit. Toby continued to control Sue; she still had to cook to please the family. Junk came in and out, living in his mother's house and with his grandparents, Toby and Sue. Then he went to jail three times for drinking and drugs. Cary brought her child to babysit, which was Toby's idea; he thought he had to do a favor for his granddaughter, who needed help, even though Sue and Toby were much older than Cary, in addition to the fact that Sue was sick and abused and should not have had to do any cooking or babysitting.

"They have no remorse for their mother," May often said. She thought their father should help their children to grow and be whatever they wanted to be. She thought, "Parents do not owe children, children owe their parents." Couldn't they see their mother was sick? And didn't they know their mother was being abused by their father? The brother and sister were only looking at their own world, only themselves. Why couldn't they ask their dad, "What happened? She was doing fine when we saw her the other day."

Dan and Lake ignored people who scolded them for not knowing how their mom was. Lake only tried to tell people that Sue is her mom. Once again, Lake had time alone with May; she defended herself to May, saying, "She is my mom," letting May know she was watching and mocking her. How sick minded she was for not seeing the person was living silently. Everyone knew Sue was Lake's mom, but May did not understand why she had to defend herself, again and again, and let May know that Sue was her mom.

Chapter 5
Now I Know

Another day, May and Joe visited Sue and Toby and brought dinner for them both. Last time, they brought her favorite, pizza, and this time they brought his favorite, fried chicken with mashed potatoes. After dinner, they went to the living room; as always, Toby started talking about poor people. He started to argue in front of May and Joe, and like every visit, he had to be the center of attention. He said, "The Mexicans are coming into this country and taking our jobs from us!"

May was not sad, rather she felt sorry for Toby. These ideas were coming from Junk, who lived with Toby and Sue. Junk was always complaining that Mexicans do this and do that. Therefore, he lost his job. May and Joe tried to ignore it. Toby knew that it did not bother May as much as it bothered Joe. Then he said that Japanese cars had overtaken American-made cars. May had had enough; she could not take his derogatory comments that "Mexicans do that" and "Japanese don't that."

As he spoke, he looked over at Joe to see his reaction to his comment. She began to get agitated; she felt assaulted by him. Her blood pressure started to go up faster than she could hold it, and her heartbeat got faster too; she had to control her anger. But she could not hold anger—she had say to him something.

However, that was Toby's plan: he wanted to get May and Joe mad and angry.

Shortly, no one wanted to hear his rabble-rousing comments. She said to Toby, "That is not true! Mexicans did not take jobs from anybody, and Japanese people did not take jobs from Americans. And stop saying 'Jap'—that is not nice! I am from Korea!"

Toby heard this and became wild, trying to point his finger at May. "How do you know? You think you are so smart!"

"I am not smart, but what you say is wrong to people who come to America. Your family came from Europe. What you are doing to your wife is very wrong too! You're just not a good man."

Oh no, he was mad, and he said to May, "This is my house; I can say anything I want, and you are not going to stop me!"

His voice was getting louder and louder. May needed to get out of there; she felt unsafe. Joe tried to stop the argument from becoming a fight. Shortly, May tried to get out of the house, but Toby cornered her; there was no way to get out. Toby cornered her against the wall, and she could not get away from him. Toby was right in her face and looked like he would hit her with his big hand. She was scared but as calm as she could be, not saying anything; she just looked at him, thinking that he was not going to hit her. Joe pushed his dad away from May, thinking he might hurt her.

Joe said, "Stop! What is the matter with you? Why are you doing this? Please stop!"

Joe tried to help May and shielded her with his body. But Toby would not stop; he looked like a madman out of control—his hands were moving quickly, and then he swung his arm slowly. Joe saw this movement and pushed his dad away from May again. Toby was aggressive and belligerent. He was close to hitting her, but thank goodness he did not. Then he said to May and Joe, "Get out of my house; get out now!"

Joe said to him, and this was not believable, "Okay, we are; we are getting out!"

May and Joe hugged his mom and told her they loved her and left the house. After that, they did not see them for almost a year. That day Joe learned how much his dad loved and cared for him; he said over and over, "Now I know my real dad, whom I thought I knew."

After Joe left the house, he had to pull over to the side of the highway and take a deep breath. He said to May, "I am so sorry. I did not think my dad would be that wild and nasty to you; I am glad that he did not hurt you. I was so scared for you, and I love you. Again, I am so sorry."

May thought he was sorry that it happened in their house. It was not right for Joe to be kicked out of his parents' house. He might not be Toby's favorite son, but he and May had raised two beautiful children, outstanding grandchildren Toby could not accept regardless of who they were. Toby showed Joe and May he was not willing to listen, but he had to show with his physical daring that he was a madman. What he did not understand was, this daring madman was a blackmailer and a horrifying parasite.

Then May said to Joe, "I am so sorry that I did not know about your dad's temper. We had to leave and go home. No reason to argue with a fool."

While driving down the long road, May was quiet, but she was angry and could not express it. Tears came down her cheeks, and she tried to wipe them away so Joe would not know, but he was feeling the same as May. After the vicious attack by his so-called father, all they could do was comfort each other. After that day, Joe's experience was a life of finding out who he became. His relationship with his father was gone forever. His childhood was over; Joe wanted to show his children that his father, their grandfather, was a good man, but it did not happen. Joe wanted to tell his son that his father was his hero. Husband and father to two children, he thought his father loved him, even though he had a rebellious relationship with his father. Joe found out and became aware that his father did not talk about it.

CHAPTER 6
Calling a Meeting with the Family

Sue and Toby's first child, Lake, lived with her son, Junk, forty years old, no more than three miles from Lake's daughter, Cary, forty-three, who was not married but had one child. Cary had had a baby so she could get help from the government: child support, food stamps, housing, and many other programs. Cary lived close to Grandmom and Grandfather, who babysat their great-grandchild and grandchildren. Toby and Sue had to raise their daughter's children. She was gone; having fun was the first thing on her mind. Her excuse was that having children was a mistake. She neglected her children. Lake was self-indulgent.

Sue and Toby's second child, Dan, has been married for forty years and has three boys: Bod has some kind of a job, Roy is the nicest person of all the family, and the third child was married twice and has one son. Dan is a retired airline pilot; he had a job where he flew all over the world. He was gone for two to three weeks at a time, and his wife June raised the children herself most of her life.

Joe and his wife, May, have been married thirty-five years; he was a truck driver. They have two children: Otto, married once, lives in his own home; he went to college to get a good job. Their daughter, Kay, is thirty-one, and she has been married eleven years and works in a doctor's office. Everyone believes May is the reason her children are successful. Kay and Otto each provide a roof over their heads and food for their dinner; they pay their bills on time. Any parent would be proud.

One day, Toby called his children together to have a meeting. Dan came with his wife June, Joe came with his wife May, and Lake came with Cary and Junk. Lake told her son and daughter to watch Uncle Dan and Uncle Joe as well as Aunt June and Aunt May. The first thing they decided was what to eat; they asked Aunt May if she wanted takeout Chinese food. Aunt May did not like fatty food, but she had no choice and agreed with Cary to get Chinese food. Three bags of Chinese food were too much, but they liked to eat. Lake fixed a dinner plate for Sue.

As they were eating in the living room, Dan asked his father, "What is this meeting all about?"

Toby answered with food in his mouth, "We will talk about it after we eat. It is about your mom!"

They knew what was coming. As soon as dinner was over, Toby and Lake picked up a piece of paper, sat on the couch, and looked at it. She tried to explain to him what was on the paper. Sue sat in her recliner, lost, feeling neglected by her husband along with her daughter.

Again, Dan asked Toby, "Why we are here, Dad? What do you want to talk about? I do not understand; you need to explain what you want."

Toby was looking at the paper while he tried to talk, so Lake responded.

After an hour, he tried to explain that he wanted Sue to go live in a nursing home. His excuse was that it was too much for him to take care of her, and he was tired of seeing her walker, so he put the walker into the garage. May could not believe what he was saying. He made sign gestures that he was being a whipping boy. May needed to do something to help her.

May thought sharply and quickly what to say; she wanted to save Sue. She said, "The walker is her life saver and safety so she can go around, and that walker will help protect her. It's a lifeline, and she should have that walker back!" May was as mad as she could be. Dan could not believe what May said to Toby.

Dan looked at May and said, "Thank you, I am so glad you said that to him."

But Toby and Lake were looking at pictures; they ignored what May and Dan said. June and May looked at each other's reaction to Toby and Lake; they were disturbed that he did not listen to the family. After a short moment, Cary (Lake's first child, who was raised by Sue and Toby most of her life) said to the family, "Granddad is helping Grandmam, and he is tired; he wants Grandmam to stay in nursing home, so he can get some rest, after then, she can come home."

Cary did not stop talking; she said, "She has Alzheimer's disease, and she cannot remember things." During every visit, Cary, Lake, or Toby would tell them that she had Alzheimer's disease and her heart was failing. Every time someone visited, Toby would say that is what she had; he would cry, "This is it."

After looking at photos for an hour and ignoring Sue all afternoon, Toby was crying and saying, "This is it; I am so tired from looking after her. She needs to go stay with a caregiver, but I do not know how to solve this problem."

He was crying and crying. How can a person change from happy to sad in just five seconds? As he got up, he said to the family, "I am going to bring her walker back; it is in the garage."

He brought back the walker and gave it to Sue, saying, "Here is your walker!" He looked disappointed that she got the walker back. Then he started to cry again, saying, "This is it! This is it; we are done!"

Toby was crying like a baby because he had to give her back the walker. Dan, Joe, and Lake tried to calm him down. Lake said to Dan and Joe, "I have been telling Dad he needs to take medication for stress."

Dan and Joe thought it was a good idea, but Toby argued, "I do not need medication; nothing is the matter with me!" He was in denial, thinking nothing was wrong with him.

Dan and Joe tried to tell Toby, "Stop crying! Why are you crying? At her age, it is normal to forget things; she does not have Alzheimer's disease—the doctor says so. You are panicking for nothing."

Toby told them he did not need to take medication for stress and nothing was the matter him. He said the matter was that his wife was using the walker, which she should not use; he felt she needed to go out without the walker. The problem could be worse if they argued with him about the walker. They had to stop talking about the walker before he became stressed out and had a heart attack. After all, he had already had two open heart surgeries. That day, he did not say what the meeting was all about; maybe he just wanted attention from Dan and Joe. And that night, Dan and Joe visited each other, but every chance they tried to talk, Junk was right there, one foot away, trying to snoop; he was nosy. Dan and Joe had no answer about what the meeting was about.

Sue was being sabotaged by Lake, Cary, and Junk along with Toby. In addition to that, they said she had Alzheimer's disease, which she did not have. Every day, after years of neglect by her husband, Sue wrote in a little notebook, "Is this marriage going to work or not?" Before she died, she wanted to say her marriage was demeaning, but she could not say how unhappy she was. She wrote in language that was so strong, but her children did not see it. Many times when May came to visit Sue, Lake would say, "She is my mom!" What was she telling May? Was she trying to tell her Sue was her mom, do not take her away from Lake? May knew Sue was Lake's mother, but Sue was also Joe and Dan's mother. May did not think that she was her mom. May did not call Sue her mom, but she often called her "Grandmother." After all, Sue was grandmother to her children, Otto and Kay. May did not cross the boundary.

Toby would come into the living room, and then she would go back to the kitchen, if not outside. There were times she and May could not avoid each other; Lake watched her and would say, "He is my dad!" She let May know that she was watching her and mocking her again; she did not want her mother and father to choose May over her. She made sure to tell her son, Junk, to watch Dan and Joe and see what they were talking about; Junk was watching to see if they were doing something that they should not do; what was it?

CHAPTER 7
Good-Bye to Sue

May and Joe were on a long drive on the road, they stopped to eat fast food and had no choice other than just fries and greasy hamburgers. May was not hungry, Joe and Otto ate fries and cheeseburgers, but it was quiet. As they ate, they were choking, trying not to show their weakness and acting like nothing happened, but she could see water in their eyes, which they tried to wipe with napkins and blow their noses.

After two days went by, Dan called Otto to say that Sue was moved to life support. Her health was failing fast and nobody could stop her—not her husband, her sons, her daughter, or her grandchildren and great-grandchild. She wanted to go, she had to go. No doubt they were thinking that her health was failing. The following weekend, Joe and May went to see Sue. As soon as they entered the room, they saw the memorabilia for her.

Toby was glad to see them; he cried and tried to wake Sue up, shaking her with his big farmer's hands, saying to her, "Joe and May are here, say hi to them."

May said to Toby, "Let her be, she does not have to say anything." May walked softly beside her and gave her a hug and said to Sue, "I love you, Grandmother." May could see that Sue had kept the teddy bear that she and Joe had given her. Joe and May had brought the teddy bear to comfort her. Every time she was in the hospital, May brought flowers or home-cooked noodles. Sue had been in and out of the hospital time after time. This teddy bear must have comforted her.

Family and friends greeted Sue and said how sorry they were, that she will be remembered. Every time someone visited, Toby would tell her, "They are coming to see you, say hi to them!" It was extremely discomforting for her to hear his voice as she lay on her deathbed. When their friends T. and J. visited, he was happy to see them and went over to Sue, shaking her with his big farmer's hands, making sure she could hear his loud voice saying, "T. and J. are here; say hi to them." She did not care nor she did know who was coming or going; she wanted to sleep in if she could. May saw all the action, she wanted to tell Toby to back off and let her be. But she did not have the right to say anything. Toby knew he needed to explain Sue's silence to T. and J. He looked at his friend's wife and said, "Come over and sit on my lap; he can talk to them, and I will tell you all about it."

May and Joe looked at each other; they did not want to talk to the man. May and Joe acted like it was painful to look at his face, they did not know what he was trying to say. Every word he said was a joke. They sat there quietly and tried not to be bothered by the inconvenience.

Lake was there with her daughter Cary to see Sue. The small hospital room was not a place to be happy or joyful or to make friends. T. and J. were talking and laughing with Toby, asking what had happened to Sue; he was not genuine, he looked sad in his face and said he was sorry for Sue. Lake could not take her father's actions and excused herself to get lunch. She left while her daughter stayed beside her grandmother. When Cary went into the bathroom, May saw something remarkable: Sue was waving exquisitely to her.

Why was she waving? May thought. *Is it to say good-bye?* May had a lump in her throat, almost uncontrollable. Then Cary came out from the bathroom and saw Sue's hand waving to May; Cary gently grabbed her hand under her blanket and then asked May, "Why she is waving at you?" May thought this question was revolting, spiteful, and hateful. Intense anger raged through her veins; she struggled not to cry. May needed to get out of Sue's room, she could not hear or see Toby neglecting Sue and giving her the cold shoulder. They did not know she was waving at May and saying good-bye to everyone in the room. If not, she was saying good-bye to May and take care.

May learned that not all closed eyes are asleep, nor are all opened eyes seeing. Sue might be in bed sleeping, but she could hear all that they said, and Toby could not see Sue wave her hand good-bye to family and friends.

That night May could not sleep or eat. She was awake all night, thinking she would hear from Dan or Lake calling Otto to say his great-grandmother Sue had ended her life. Why didn't he call his brother Joe? The complexity between the two brothers was incomprehensible. May asked herself why Sue was smiling, what was she trying to tell her? May tried not to think about her last smile the day she visited.

They all thought she was going to be okay. Lake went out to get a pizza for lunch. May did not understand how she could be hungry for pizza; her mother was lying in bed without moving, and pizza was Sue's favorite food to eat. Why would they eat pizza in front of her? They could order other food, chicken or something else. She might not be smiling but she was breathing and alive. It was hard-headed, not sentimental, a person's life is priceless; Sue had given birth and love to her family.

Joe was angry that Lake brought pizza for lunch; he could not eat any pizza that day. He was also angry because Toby had explained to his friends that Sue had the hiccups, which caused her heart attack. Joe could not accept this story. She had spent her life taking care of him and sharing love; wouldn't he be missing her? Joe was loved and care for by her, making emptiness, sadness, and tears in his heart; he could not explain it other than to say, "I love you, Mom; sorry you have to go."

The next day, Dan called to say Sue had passed away at eight o'clock in the morning. We all knew she wanted to go and nobody could stop her. She would not be forgotten. Where was Toby's morality? While Sue was dying, fighting for her last breath in her life, he was holding hands with his woman friend and trying to explain to her that hiccups had caused Sue's heart attack. Three months ago, when she was in the hospital after falling on her back, the doctor explained to him she was doing okay. She did not have a heart problem, and she was going to be okay. He forgot all the promises he made to her. And a man's best possession is a sympathetic wife. Where is a sympathetic wife, he call love?

To Miss Sue:

They see your eyes closed; I see your eyes wide open.

They see your motion is no longer alive; I see your motion is alive and loved by me.

You have been neglected and abused a long time; they are in denial about your neglect.

I saw the truth, what happened: you were abused by someone you thought you knew and loved.

I saw the truth in your beautiful smile; I saw you give me, with your last energy, a good-bye. I saw you are alive.

I must carry on; you are truly missed.

This poem is dedicated to Miss Sue from Miss May, who truly misses her and hopes that Joe and May can carry on her love; they loved Sue. After all, she was the nicest person who lived, but where is her so-called husband? Ominously and fearfully, her loved ones are in denial and do not see it as shameful. May said, "I am not her daughter, but she is grandmother to my children and mother to Joe my husband; I have a right to say I loved her, and I am not trying take her away from Lake. Lake does not have to say over and over to Miss May, 'She is my mother!'"

Sue was also mother to Dan and Joe, and May knew she was not her mother, but May respected Sue just as she cared for her own mother, and May knew both mothers loved May for the responsible person she became.

CHAPTER 8
One Rotten Apple Went Overseas

Toby began his journey in Pearl Harbor. In a large cargo ship, five hundred or more soldiers were packed like sardines, legs squeezed tight. They gasped fresh air to breathe. Some were proud to be there, and some were lost, asking where they were going. Some had answers, and some did not. Some were chatting, some were reading, and some were sleeping. Some were making friends, and some were talking about where they came from and whether they had a high school sweetheart they had to let go. The breeze from the coast had a texture of sea salt. A gentle clicking, humming, and squeaking noise came from the cargo ship, getting louder and louder; they looked at each other, and it was time to rest. Sitting for long hours, their legs needed to be stretched, but there was no room to move around. Young soldiers began to tire and get homesick. One by one, they began to lay down their heads, using their bags as pillows. It was not soft or lumpy.

Toby was a young soldier; he was walking with a friend from his hometown, laughing and giggling, looking for pretty ladies to get their attention. Shortly, some ladies were walking down the sidewalk and yelling at him, "Why aren't you fighting this war? Pearl Harbor was attacked by Japan. Why are you here? We need you to protect us, young man!" The ladies were screaming for help. He was afraid, fighting and mystified, and bewildered as he contemplated. Without warning, he ran into a wall; he could not get out and could not back off. Hastily, he screamed to another soldier, "Move over, man, I need my leg room." Toby was screaming that it did not matter how but he needed to get out of the street. He did not know what he was saying or doing; he was just glad that he was away from the wall.

Toby was sweating and fighting; as he opened his eyes, there was his drill sergeant standing over him, looking at the young soldier and asking, "What is the matter, soldier?"

"Nothing is the matter, DS, I just need my leg room!" The young soldier told the DS, "He is too close to me, and I need a little room to move around."

The DS was getting irritated by the young soldier's crying. DS began to discipline Toby; he asked, "How old are you, @#@# soldier?"

"Eighteen years old," Toby answered with pride.

DS asked, "Do you know where you are going, @#@# soldier?"

"I do not know, DS," he said.

"We are at war; Japan has attacked us. We have to fight for our country—do you understand, @#@# soldier? When you fight for the country, you will share with other soldiers—do understand, @#@# soldier?"

"No, DS," Toby said, "I do not know how to share. Why do I have share with a n—? My dad taught me that the n—s are no good and I should not share with them!"

DS could not believe what he was hearing. He grabbed a black soldier and asked him, "Are you no good, soldier?"

The black soldier answered with pride, "No, DS, sir. I am a good soldier, sir, and I am fighting for this country, sir, and I will protect the citizens of the United States, DS, sir."

The DS pointed to the other soldier again and asked loudly, "Is this soldier no good?"

Every soldier answered loudly, "No, sir, he is a good soldier, DS, sir." They echoed with one voice, a rousing sound from nearly all of them.

You could hear the cargo ship humming and cranking. Kind words can be short and easy to speak, but their echoes are truly endless. It was a long road; it was the duty and responsibility of each soldier to respect other soldiers of all colors. DS let go of the black soldier and said, "You can sit down, soldier!"

The soldier answered politely, "Thank you, sir, DS, sir!"

"Do not thank me—thank the United States of America!"

"Yes sir, DS, sir!" The black soldier was as proud as he could be with his dignity. He sat down quietly and quickly, with a good feeling about what he heard; it gave him hope in the future.

DS could see Toby needed to be criticized. He began to drill Toby. "Give me two hundred pushups! You will do what I tell you—do you understand, soldier?"

"Yes, DS." Toby began to do pushups.

DS explained what he should and should not do:

1. You will answer with "Yes, sir" when answering a superior.

2. You will protect this country with your effort.

3. You will kill the enemy to save your country; you will kill or be killed.

4. You will respect your commander.

5. You will not complain if you are hurt.

"Do you understand, soldier?"

"Yes sir, DS, sir!" Toby learned how say to "yes, sir" to superior officers. He sat down carefully, trying not to bother anyone, thinking that his tongue-lashing and criticism were humiliating; he could not comprehend it. He thought to himself, *I gave n— hope in the future but sent myself down to hell.*

Toby also learned that, to a soldier, the rifle was a best friend. And training in boot camp began in earnest. The young man understood that he needed to follow the rules. He cautiously lay in his bag, thinking, missing home as well as friends. He was now in the military and had to obey to survive. Though it was a hardship, he knew that when he got out of the military, he would be accepted as a hero. He looked to the future and wanted to marry and have children. At the same time, he was dreaming of the farm, having farm equipment of his own like a tractor to cut the corn. As he closed his eyes, he slept deep, dreaming of flying in the sky; he dropped into the cornfield, running through it to a girl he liked and was glad to see. She was beautiful and blonde, her soft lips were so sweet, and he told her, "I love you, and I miss you."

"Where have you been, Toby?" she asked.

"I was in the military, and now I am home; will you marry me?"

It was a dream, a sweet dream. As he turned around, he realized that he could not—he must not—complain, and he must be a good boy. But did he? He knew the church the family went to, but they ignored him and acted like nothing was the matter. He was displeased and intended to leave the family church. He wondered why. He did not have an explanation or commentary. In his world, everyone was under fire, but not him.

One rotten apple poisoned with toxins cannot be trusted. A brave man is not afraid to admit his mistakes; if a man cannot admit his mistakes, then he is a coward. Heroes do not say, "I am a hero, and you must pay attention to me and call me a hero." Instead, they protect their country and the people they love, and they share and help those with next to nothing. They do what they are asked, and they do not want attention—it is unnecessary; instead, they give more to their country and to those they love. They do not call themselves heroes.

CHAPTER 9
Island to Island and a Scapegoat

Toby was on some island. It was completely out of his world. People lived in small houses made with hay, and the roof was also made with hay. The weather was hot and muggy, farmers worked with their hands, and one cow would pull a wooden plow. He did not see any women. No children were playing outside. He was lost, but making friends. And three young men were with him; they came from the country like he did, and they got along with each other and were eager to work together. Wherever they went, they were together. Before they knew it, they became lifelong friends.

Some were busy building the tents, and others were cooking. Most of them had never cooked or built a shed before. Their first meal was mashed potatoes, meatloaf, and green beans. It seemed almost as good as Mom's home cooking, but soldiers were hungry from working and building tents to stay dry. There was not much going on in that part of the country. It was as quiet as any other countryside. You could hear cows mooing from the other side of the country. Once in a while, a dog barked. Every house had a private fence. In the night, nothing happened; people stayed in their home with their family. In the night, they would go out to the city; it was their favorite time, for the soldiers enjoyed having fun with the go-go girls.

Toby was single, like his two friends. They went out once a week, sometimes twice. Every woman they met was beautiful and smart. It was 1946, during World War II. The government had to control the young GIs, who were often homesick. In most of Asia, the government provided go-go girls, and those girls could provide an income to their family. The war killed many honest people; many children lost their mom or dad. Many were single parents. Some were lucky and married soldiers and came to America, but many wanted to go back home. The reason was many got married for the wrong reason, but some did not give up and they stayed with a soldier because they thought they knew how to raise children.

But Toby did not care; the only thing on his mind was to finish the war and go home a hero to his family. He was a patriot; no doubt he loved America. He loved it so much, but he could not stand people of other colors or races; overall, he made himself a bold, heroic soldier that could overcome anyone in his way. In South Asia, along the Tropic of Capricorn and equator, warm weather can bring rain for two to three hours, or the muggy weather can be very uncomfortable if you come from cold weather. The daily life of a soldier was busy as a bee. They would deliver equipment to other compounds or bring equipment back from other compounds. On the weekend, they had a chance to meet beautiful women, and many soldiers made them their girlfriend. Toby had brought a photo of his girlfriend from home, showing that girlfriend sitting on his lap. The three young soldiers were always working together, going out together, sleeping in the same tent, and eating together. And they had the same thought as patriots.

One day, Toby got a letter from his mom saying that his young brother, who played the trumpet in the high school band, was dating his girlfriend. He was disappointed, but he did not care;

he had another girlfriend who was more beautiful than his high school girlfriend. He wanted to marry that girl and bring her to America. In a few days, he planned to ask her. Sunday came along, and he was with his girlfriend. His mental condition was muddled, because if he asked her, she would ask him, "Why do you want to marry me?" He could not explain why he wanted to marry her, and he could not tell her that the letter from his mom was the cause. But he was dating before he left. He wanted to be a hero and an honorable soldier when he got back to home. But what he wanted did not happen. Too much for a good soldier, but was what he was saying true?

The following week, he wrote a letter to his mom, saying he had his eye on this girl he liked; he wanted to hear from her and asked his mom to ask her to write him. His mom did ask her to write to him. She was excited and wrote to him that she would like to see him as soon as he came home. He wrote back that he would be home soon. He wanted the attention as if he was a hero, since he never got attention from any of his family or friends, but he had a lot of attention from every woman he met while he was in Japan.

He was helping to deliver equipment; there was nothing to write about when he was overseas, but he had a picture of a woman he'd been carrying all his life. He did not explain to the family who that woman was. There were many things he kept to himself. Back then, black and white soldiers had to sleep in different sections of the room, and at dinner, the whites ate first before black soldiers could sit at the dining table.

And he used bad language when he talked about black people, saying, "Damn n—s are taking my job!" and "Damn n—s do that!" May was tired of hearing the "N" word; it irritated her after many years.

When he came home from the military, his mother had to hide his gun in the closet so he could not get it. In some sense, his mother was mad and she thought he might be in hot water if she did not hide that gun. Four months after he came home, he and the object of his affection began to date. They became girlfriend and boyfriend, and they planned to get married. His mother wanted him to marry soon. At that time, Miss Sue made herself a wedding dress. They got married before they knew each other; they did not want a big wedding like his brother or sister. There were few people in the little church; his brother, a minister, officiated as they promised to tie the knot.

When he dreamed of two young people getting married, he didn't think the dream would ever be realized. Again, he came home a hero, and his family and church members could not give him the attention and praise he wanted. They did not see him with admiration, as a war hero.

A real patriot is the fellow who gets a parking ticket and is glad that the system works. He never asks himself who he is. "If he can change thoughts, then he could change the world and open it to the direction where he wants to go."

CHAPTER 10
Begin with a First Child

Marriage brings children; two people join their lives and, with their love, hope in the future. All mothers try to protect their children, but a man cannot always control his sexual drive. A woman's purity is questionable; all men should have some education about women, and at the same time, women should learn about men, dealing with a degree of dignity and sobriety.

Toby had hid his sexual drive; he had to have sex every day. He did not have an intimate relationship with his wife; he was a craven and pusillanimous man. Sixty-five years ago, when Sue was pregnant with Lake, she could not give Toby the attention he wanted. He started to show his real demoralizing personality, showing that he looked for sexual attraction from other women. He could not get sexual attention at that moment, so he turned to adultery. A man should show he is the man; he should get what he wants, overpowering the woman, and let the man control his wife and children; good or bad, this gives power to the man. With that, wives are thinking he will come home and then everything will be all good. But Toby had a problem mentally, having nightmares about his time overseas. It must have been hard; he sweated and wet the bedsheets and screamed out.

One night, Toby had a dream about his father being ready to butcher a cow and take it to a slaughter house. The slaughter house was one mile from his house. When they got to the slaughter house, then his father showed Toby how to slice the cow's throat; at that moment, the blood spilled all over him, and his father looked at Toby and said, "Okay, son, now you try it." They brought another cow and stood in front of him; the cow mooed, and when young Toby heard mooing, he saw the cow's big brown eyes were crying; young Toby thought, *Do I have to slaughter this cow?*

He looked at his father's face and made eye contact; his father was saying, "Do it; if you do not, then we might not have steak for dinner." Toby did not want to go hungry when he went to bed, so he grabbed the knife from his father's hand and tried to cut the cow's throat, but he could not reach it; he was too short, but his father looked at him, coldhearted; he was teaching his child how to be strong and become a man of the house. Toby was taught by his father, showing his son what he should become, as he learned from his father, saying, "My dad showed me how to kill a cow; I am going to show you what my dad showed me."

Then his father grabbed his son, lifted him up, and told Toby to cut the cow's throat. Toby was scared, but he knew if he did not do what his dad told him, then he would have to face the consequences: punishment was spanking with a leather belt. Toby grabbed the knife, his feet were dangling in the air, thinking in his mind he did not want to be spanked by his father, at the same time, he swung the knife, but he could not look at the cow's big innocent eyes, as he swung the slaughtering knife, his eyes were shut.

He swung the knife and thought he did a good job; he proudly asked his father, "Did I do okay, Father?" But when he opened his eyes, he saw the cow was not bleeding, the knife had cut his dad's cheek, Toby's dad dropped his son under the slaughtering table, young Toby asked for help and looked at his dad's face, there was blood all over his hand, his dad pulled him over the top of the table and told him to get help. The young boy was crying and ran screaming for help; he ran in to Mom. He could not stop crying; his mother asked, "Why are you crying? Stop crying and tell me what has happened."

"I cut Dad's face, and he needs help. Please, Mom, help, help!"

"Okay, son, we'll get help; it should be all right."

His dad had twelve stitches on his cheek. After that, Toby became an isolated young boy with a difficult life and a learning problem in school.

When Lake, Toby and Sue's first child, was born, Toby was as happy as he could be. But his mind was not washed away from his fear and adultery. As time went by, every so often, he had a nightmare about his military experience. And his overseas girlfriend was hanging around; he taught himself how to control his sexual drive and not be overexposed to the high demands of his sexual drive. Lake was the center of attention; she was beautiful, playful, loveable, and huggable. Sometimes, he took a nap with her. She grew like a bean sprout. Their relationship as father and daughter also grew. Toby often told his young daughter, "My sweet, sit on my lap," and she would.

As a little girl, Lake did not know about getting attention from her father; she hopped into her father's lap and chatted with him about what she wanted to be when she grew up. As she talked, he looked like he was listening, but in reality, it was in a sexual way that these conversations pleased him. It must have been going on until she no longer played on his lap.

Life went on, and Toby and Sue wanted to have another child.

Their second child came along, a son, and their life was a big deal. Dan was playful with his mother. But Toby continued with his perpetual sexual drive, and he wanted to continue play time with his daughter sitting on his lap. Dan did not talk much with Toby. He was quiet, and his dad commented that he was the apple of his mother's eye.

Toby was the third generation of his family to live in the country; they had a farm and raised most of their food. The food came from irrigated land, butchered meat, and vegetables, potatoes, and many other things they canned for winter. He came from pioneers from Germany three generations ago. His grandfather bought cheap farmland. They broke the ground without any modern equipment, but Toby's grandfather grew corn and soy beans like many others. Two people came to America with two children, and their family had grown. But Toby did not see that his grandfather started this country with new ideas, hope and love of whom he wanted to grow proud; one of his relatives wanted to be an innkeeper.

Many cousins had success, but Toby chose to be who he wanted to be, and he should not have been around children. Every mother should pay attention so that their children are comfortable with their grandfather or father.

CHAPTER 11
Toby Says He Wants Another Girl, Not Another Boy

After Dan was born, Toby and Sue had another boy, Joe. Toby said to his wife, "I want to have another little girl, not a boy with a little weeny!" Sue could do nothing; the child was here, and she could not send him back where he came from. She explained, "He's just a little baby, he can grow like you are, and he is quiet."

Joe grew like any other boy. He and Dan played together and went to school together; they were buddies and best friends, Joe thought. Like all boys, they would get into trouble. After all, Toby was never there to help with their homework or play any sports with them. He had an excuse: he had no time because he was working. His job was selling used cars; he also worked as a janitor and as a farmer growing corn. He could not stay in one job more than five months. One day, when Toby came home, Sue told him that the boys had been in the neighbor's yard; he wanted to know what the boys were doing, and he was looking for an excuse to pick on them.

Sue said they were in the kitchen; the two brothers knew what was coming, but they were smiling and smirking like smart alecks. When Toby saw the boys were smart asses, he pulled out his leather belt and told them to take down their pants. In a moment, their pants were down. He began to whip their tender skin; he told the boys, "You're laughing at me? I'll show you how to laugh!"

He whipped them and whipped them; by this time, the two boys were in tears and said to their father, "We will not cross the neighbor's yard again; you can stop, Dad!"

He whipped them harder; Sue saw that the boys were hurt and asked him to stop. He stopped and told the boys, "If you laugh again, next time will hurt more, do you understand?"

"Yes, Dad, we understand."

They ran into their room and stayed there until dinnertime. At this time, Joe had a learning problem and physical issues, beginning with a hernia that he developed when he was three years old. Then he had to wear eyeglasses. He was not a good student like Dan or Lake; he was a slow learner and left handed.

When he was in second grade, the teacher saw him writing with his left hand. She tried to teach him to write with his right hand, but when Joe tried to write with his right hand, he could not do it. He went back to writing with his left. The teacher whipped him with her yardstick, saying, "I am telling you, write with your right hand!" Joe tried it again with his right hand, but he could not do it. The teacher came back with the yardstick, saying, "How many times do I have to tell you, write with your right hand!" The teacher whipped his hand, over and over on top of his hand. He went home with a bruised and swollen hand.

At dinnertime, when Joe's mother saw his hand, she asked, "What happened to your hand?"

"A teacher hit me with her yardstick because I write with my left hand, Mom." He burst into tears.

Toby looked at young Joe's hand and face; it did not matter that he got hit by a teacher. But his mother was not going to let a chicken-hearted teacher pick on her son. The next day, Sue went to the school and confronted the teacher (later, after Dan married June, they learned that Joe's teacher was her grandmother); Sue said, "It is wrong for a teacher to hit a child's hand because he is left handed; please do not hit my child's hand anymore." But that did not help young Joe's learning in school; at the same time, he was out with a hernia operation, making Joe gain weight; he became bigger than his brother and sister.

A few years later, Joe realized that his father would not pay attention to him like he needed. He started to take care of many things himself. He started working when he was eight years old; he earned money to buy shoes and clothes, for lunch, and for spending money. His first job was picking rocks in the cornfield; it made him twenty to forty dollars. For a young man, having twenty to forty dollars was a lot to spend. He began to have a passion for model cars. He began buying model cars and spending hours putting them together, enjoying himself in the basement, where they stored junk and other things.

One day he bought some model cars for himself with his paycheck, like any other day. He had lots of model cars on the shelf. As always, once school was out, he went home to play with his model cars; he wanted to put together the newest car he bought; he was having a daydream that he would like to have a real car. He rushed home, his father was home and burning garbage in the wheelbarrow; he said to his father, "Hi Dad, you home early?" Joe ran down to the basement but didn't see any of his model cars; all the models car were gone. He had put time and love into building all those cars, but they were gone, just disappeared into the air; there was nothing.

Joe panicked, became mad and bewildered, and ran out and asked his father, "My model cars are all gone, what happened to my model cars, Dad?"

Joe was crying; he thought his father could help him find the model cars. Toby smirked and looked grimly at him; he said, "I am burning your model cars!"

"What! Why?"

"You take too much space with your model cars!"

Joe tried to grab what he could, but it was too late. All the model cars were melting like rubber. He ran into his room crying, feeling lost and hurt mentally and emotionally, his young, tender heart scarred forever. What kind of father would take away his son's dream?

Joe looked to replace the way he felt about the cars; three months later, he adopted a little dog and named it Spice. He could not get attention from his father or mother. Dan was a smart child and got attention from his father and mother, he had a lot of friends; Lake was always getting attention from her father because she was Daddy's little girl. Spice became Joe's best friend and gave Joe all the attention he needed. They went fishing, they took walks, and they played together. Spice loved Joe more than anyone in the family.

One day, Joe's English teacher called (the same one who did not like Joe using his left hand to write). The teacher called his mother and said, "Mrs. Sue, you need to pick up this dog; this dog belongs to Joe! This dog is starting to bark, and the children cannot pay attention in class."

The next day, Sue told Toby that the English teacher had called; Spice followed Joe and went to school. Spice knew when Toby was home; he hid until Joe came home. That day Spice was not thinking clearly, wagging his tail and trying to become friendly to Toby, but Toby had something else in mind, saying, "I will show you your wagging tail!" He grabbed Spice and took him to the dog pound, saying he was a stray.

As always, when Joe came home from school, he looked for Spice; he called him, thinking he might have found a place to hide. He looked in the shed and called, "Hi Spice, I'm home, you'll be okay, come out!"

There was no Spice. Toby came in from outside and asked Joe, "What are you looking for? You looking for Spice?"

"Yes, Dad, have you seen my Spice?"

"Yes, I did, and I took him to the dog pound! You have a problem, son?"

"Why did you do that? He was good dog and my best friend!" Joe knew he must not complain; the more he complained, the more he'd get a whipping.

He was only eleven years old, but he had to provide money for food and school clothes; he had to get a job picking rocks in the cornfield, and in the summertime he worked at a gas station washing car windows. It was just too much responsibility for a young man. May wondered, *How can a father choose one child over another child? Every child should be paid attention by parents equally, loved and given the opportunity to learn; parents should not belittle any child.*

Where were Toby's principles? Didn't he know how to be a father? Didn't he know a father should teach his children, not hurt their heart? Didn't he have a father's fundamental personal code of conduct? What kind of father was he? Every child wants to learn that their father is their hero and grow up to be like their father. He could show his vision to his child, and he must show how much he cared. Instead, Toby showed his children, grandchildren, and great-grandchildren he was a damnable person, abusive and a loser. It was his road, bad or good, it had no motive. He could not understand what he had done to his family, that his perfectionism made him a bad parent.

Toby would tell friends and family, "I wanted to have another little girl, but I got another boy."

Joe said to May, "I do not need to explain at all; the world knows what that means."

"What difference is a boy or girl?" Miss May asked. "For him, having another girl would add more fun to his life." She had no questions to ask. She knew what he was trying to say.

CHAPTER 12
Where Is the Law?

Every father knows when his daughter gets sexual attention from boys. Toby closely watched Lake and carefully planned how to proceed to get his sexual needs from her; like someone who fell in love with his reflection in the water, being a narcissist and thick skinned and hard hearted, he had no mercy. One night, it was a perfect night with moonlight shining in the window; he closed his eyes and saw the reflection of go-go girls from overseas. Then he knew he needed attention to his sexual drive. He had been controlling his ill-natured and ill-tempered sexual attention, and his wife did not give him pleasure. That night, Sue was tired and snoring away. He looked at her and was no longer sexually attracted to her; instead, his mind was on how to get close to his daughter. It was the perfect night for him to get close to her.

He acted like he was going to the bathroom and snuck into Lake's room; he lay beside her and whispered softly into her ear, "I am going to help show you how to have an intimate relationship with a boy."

Lake was scared but asked, "How are you going to show me?"

"Well, the first time you are intimate with a boy can be uncomfortable; it can hurt if the boy you are dating is no good and does not know how to do it, and I am going to go easy on your vagina. Next time you do it with a boy, it will be fun and easier, okay, my sweet? I love you, and that is why I am doing this—just relax and I will take care of it."

Lake did not know how to react to Toby's big hand that was touching her; Toby told her, "You are my best child, and I will take care of you."

Lake had no choice but let Toby do it; if not, she might get hurt by him. She was scared and said, "Okay, Dad, you can do that, but easy, Dad, I love you, Dad."

"I love you too, dear."

He said it was consensual, between father and daughter, and he was not hasty. He penetrated her vagina quickly and unfaithfully. His little girl was scared and lost, hurt, and muddled; her confidence and innocence were broken by a sick, nasty, dirty, filthy man. After that night, Lake became the attention of his sex drive for life. Whenever Lake needed things, she'd get them from her dad. They began to have sex with each other all the time. She believed that he would take care of what she needed. Time went faster, and she graduated from high school.

Lake first married a young man, but it did not last long—less than three years. She had a problem with men. Toby did not like any man she dated or married. He did not want to let go of her. He was thinking she could take the place of his long-time lover overseas, but he had a bad memory from overseas. Every time he thought of sex when he dreamed, he became a child in the butcher shop. When he was in the army overseas, he lost his virginity to a go-go girl. He loved them and dealt only with social matters. One day he was on duty with his buddies. It was a beautiful moonlit night; the silky wind touching his skin made him dream of going home. Soon they saw an old man walking beside the fence, minding his own business; he had been drinking and saw the young soldiers, who he thought were friendly, and asked, "Hi soldiers, how you guys doing?"

It was a mistake for the friendly old man to say hi. The young soldiers thought that he was there to spy on them, they were also lonely and missing their family, they were angry and bullied the old man, who did not understand how lonely the life of a soldier was. Instead of being friendly, the soldiers became extremely hurtful and took the old man's life. Toby and the two others pointed their guns at the old man. But the old man was drunk and thought the soldiers were playing; he said, "I mean you no harm."

But Toby and his two friends did not hear what the old man said; instead, they said, "What did you say, old punk? Are you spying on us, you foolish old man?" They started beating the old man with their rifles, kicking and punching with their big farmer's hands; the old man screamed, and the more he screamed, the madder Toby got. He told him to shut up, the old man was dying from being beaten, then Toby shot the old man with his gun. Then they let him die.

After serving overseas for one year, Toby came home with nightmares; he often woke up sweating and screaming for help. He told Sue what happened that night. All three children could hear him screaming in the night many times; Joe asked his mother what all that screaming was about; she told him what happened overseas, that Toby killed an old man and now he was having nightmares about that night. The dream was so vivid. In war there is no law. Yes, he killed a person but it was not related to the war. And now he was a sexual pervert. There was no excuse to have bad dreams, rape your child, and kill a man with obnoxious hatred.

But where is the law? Some say, if you do not speak, then who is going to speak up? There is no excuse to not speak up. We must say what happened to a child raper or an outrageous killer with malicious corruption. As a mother, May could not stand by and support him without speaking up. She must not sweep it under the rug and act like nothing was the matter. But he ignored the law and thought that he was the law in this family and taught them how they could become unpleasant, annoying, objectionable to others and discriminate against those of different colors. Miss May was sick and did not want her children to go see their grandfather.

You might ask May, "How do you know that story is true, that he really did that? What kind of evidence or proof do you have?"

You may remember, once when Joe was in high school, when Toby was having a nightmare, screaming and sweating, Joe was there to help. And Sue told Joe, Dan, and Lake what happened overseas when he was guarding the fence with two other soldiers. One of those friends had died, and the other was alive five years ago and visited with Dan; he drove to another state and saw him.

Chapter 13
Joe Grows into a Young Man and Finds a Wife

Dan was the smartest of Toby and Sue's children. He did well in high school and went to university and became a pilot; he married June and had three boys. They moved from state to state and lived in different parts of the country. The military gave him a good life; with his job, he flew all over the world, had a nice home, and could retire with a good pension. Overall, he was Toby's favorite son.

Joe saw his sister get married and move to another state, and then his brother went into the military and became an officer. He wondered what his future could be. He thought to himself about when his English teacher called him evil because he wrote with his left hand. And a math teacher violated the limits of learning by telling Joe he had to play on the basketball team or else he would fail math. One day, the math teacher asked him if he could play basketball. He tried playing basketball, but he was not good at it. He discovered that playing basketball was not something he did well. The school needed players and the teacher encouraged students to play. Joe did not understand; the only thing on his mind was he needed to get off the basketball team. And he needed to go to work, so he could provide for himself. But he could not quit because the math teacher told him, "If you do not play, then you are going to fail your math classes!" The teacher failed him in math class that year, when he was only eleven years old. He could not get help from his father or mother or siblings. He began to panic about failing the math classes, and then he began to stutter; he could not control or overcome his panic attacks. He struggled and had difficulty constructing and organizing sentences. He made himself believe in his dream and graduated from high school. He joined the military; that was the only way to get out from under his father's wing. Joe was proud to become a soldier; he was as happy as a little puppy and had the chance to travel overseas. He thought to himself, *I hope to find my wife there.* He was determined to find a wife before he went home.

Japan controlled almost all of Asia, and the Japanese government did not want to educate Korea and other countries. As a resort, Japan gave it up. Then the Korean War began, and it lasted almost five years. The war brought unemployment; many children were raised without both parents. The government did provide go-go girls to help families earn money and to help young soldiers. When Joe arrived overseas, he was in heaven. There were so many beautiful girls, he thought he was in a story out of Hollywood. He went out every day he could and met new friends. Most of all he sent money home to his mother, so she could save it in his bank account. At that time, she was working at a bank; he thought he could trust his mother and thought she would save the money in his name. That did not happen, and he found out later that the money was gone; he had no money in his bank account. In March 1973, Joe met May, his future wife. He thought he had never, ever seen such a beautiful woman in his life. May had graduated from high school and was looking for some adventure. A friend's big sister had a go-go club and was looking for girls to work for her. May went to high school with that girl and she was her best friend. May's best friend took her to the go-go club. May was ninety pounds and five feet, two inches tall. She was mighty small, but she was not a harebrained girl; and no one tried to pull her leg. At the same time, she thought it would give her a chance at adventure and meet Europeans and Americans. She was not thinking she'd meet her future husband and get married. But she met Joe and got married before they had Otto, their first child. She had no choice, she had to go to America and give birth.

It was a problem for Joe. He did not come home until three months and ten days after Otto was born. He was glad to see his first son and happy to be reunited with Miss May. But he did not know that May had been dealing with a complicated issue with Toby. He thought he would marry May, and she would be accepted by his father and the family. Most of all, he thought he had won the big prize and was proud to show May to his friends and family. He thought that every problem he had with his father would go away. The big prize he won made him a big man in feeling and emotion. What Joe did not know was the dark side of his father's ego. As Joe and May wrote letters back and forth before he rejoined her in America, he learned about his father's dark side, but Joe did not want to be responsible, just to himself, to his wife, and to his son. What kind of man was his father? What kind of father would he be? And what kind of husband?

Chapter 14
May's Adventure Begins

May thought hard about what was the right thing to do with her child. At that time, the war with Japan was over, and then the Korean War was over after five long years. Every Korean parent worked hard and educated their children to graduate from high school or as far as they could go. The government took action after the war to get the people out of poverty and become independent. In the late fifties, after the war, the parents of Korean children wanted to stay within themselves. May had to think hard, if she took her child home she might not ever see him again. She had to choose to keep that child with her. She thought hard and promised Otto that they would go to America and grow together; she would teach him about her Korean grandfather and hope everything would be okay. She loved Otto more than life itself.

Coming to America is the dream of people throughout the world. May talked to her unborn child and said, "You are going to go home, and I will stand by you during the journey." She realized she was surrounded by strangers in a strange land. She was thinking she might meet Indian scalpers, like she learned from high school history how American black men became slaves. Her mind was full of wonders. As the plane touched down at Chicago Airport, she saw the bright lights miles away from the runway, and high-rise buildings were lit up with blue, red, white, and yellow colors. As she retrieved her luggage and walked into the lobby, questions came to mind: what, where, why, how was she going to fit in this environment? Her mind was blanking; the more questions she asked, the more her emotions and intelligence were dumfounded as to answer.

On the other hand, her mouth became cotton dry, and the tension merged like an electromagnetic force; from head-to-toe, she had a ghostly fear like a heavy burden on her shoulders. May embraced her fear and stood firmly on her two feet, ready to meet her in-laws. The lobby was crowded with all kinds of people. They were hurrying to other destinations; she thought she might run into an Indian chief. At the same time, she could hear multiple languages simultaneously: English, Russian, French, and some Asian. She could see the speakers express their personality along with their nationality. There were loud sounds like caterwauling and some whispers that she could not understand.

Indeed, May was exposed to the world; she did not know who she was going to meet or where she was going. May was pregnant and came to America without her husband; this was perilous and taking a risk to help her child grow; she was accountable, and he was a liability; she did not know what kind of future it was going to be. She became sick; she was a bony stick, a ninety-five-pound pregnant girl. She promised her unborn child, "I will never let you go, and I stand beside you no matter what it takes."

May's experience in Chicago Airport was eye-opening. It was her first but she did not want to have a second one. At the same time, she had mixed emotions: fear and joy. Her fear was, "What if Joe's family doe not accept us?" It was a spine-chilling thought. "But look at people of all colors, and the languages they speak; why should they not accept us?" She was positive that she could walk into lobby with no fear and with her head up, and they would say, "You made it, and your future is are here." She believed in the hope of her child.

May was thinking about the future and her plans; she did not know what would come to her child in the future. It was important; she had to do it so he could develop. In Asia, the child is first, before oneself. The mother rubs her tummy and talks to her child to prepare, to teach her child leadership, integrity, and rational intelligence. May walked solo; her solitude, her solitary isolation, seclusion, and loneliness, helped her deal with chaos, which helped her to be stronger and fulfilled. When one lets go of what it is, it becomes what might be. May's plane touched down in Chicago Airport on October 2, 1975. She was tired from her fourteen-hour flight. But she did not hurry to meet her in-laws. Toby and Sue immediately recognized her, and it was a good feeling for May. They introduced themselves to May and then walked into a sub shop in the lobby; she needed to eat some food, because she had not eaten in almost two days. The baby was asking for food, she thought. Miss May was eating as fast as she could.

Sue was worried and said to May, "Slow down, dear!" But she could not help it; she just ate and ate, without saying a word, thinking that feeding her child was the most important at that moment. Her first meal was french fried potatoes and fast food washed down with a Coke, and the fat content was the most of any food she had ever eaten. She did not care about the fat content, thinking a mother was feeding a child. At the same time, May was behaving like an angel. She smiled to both grandparents; she wanted her first impression as their daughter-in-law to be caring for their grandchild. May wanted to be accepted by Joe's family. Since her husband was not there to help, she had to do what it took to bring her child to safety. After finishing dinner, they went home. It was a five-hour drive. As soon as she got into Toby and Sue's car, May's eyes were getting tired; she lay in the back of the car and snored away. May did not know where they were going. What she could do? She had to trust Joe, and she thought she could trust his mom and dad. It was dark as they drove almost five hours to get home. When the car stopped, May woke up when she heard Toby open the trunk. Toby and Sue carried her luggage into the house. Then they took her into the house and gave her a room to sleep in. She was happy as she could be. She had thought she made it to Joe's home and met his parents. She felt secure and comforted and went back to sleep until noon. May woke to the smell of food; they were cooking fried chicken and mashed potatoes and green beans for May, waiting for her to get up from her long three-day journey.

In the next three weeks, May met all Joe's family members, cousins, uncles, and aunts; May could not remember all their names. Every day, they came to see May, Joe's wife who came from Korea. May was so proud to be Korean. One day, Toby's mother stopped by; she reminded May of her grandmother, who was also a daring person. May visited Joe's grandmother during summer vacation. Every time May visited with Joe's grandmother, she gave May nothing but approval and admiration, making her feel she was the best of all the grandchildren. May's grandmother was short and petite, and her paternal grandmother was tall with eyeglasses. Both had long silky white hair in a French braid. In essence, they were both kind, gentle, and thoughtful. They were from two different worlds: Asia and Europe, two different people who were equally charismatic, heroic, devoted, spunky, and enthusiastic; May believed she was the center of attention at a critical time.

Every time Joe's paternal grandmother visited, she taught May a lesson about her life. Most Asians are not carnivores; rather, they are vegetarian, and they eat rice and seafood. That first bite of Kentucky fried chicken is gratifying and pleasing, it indulges and satisfies. The food comforts no matter how many calories are in it; the satisfaction at that moment is the happiest feeling. When May lived overseas, she did not care about how many calories she ate; with a vegetarian diet, one does not have to count calories. So

May did not know how many calories she was eating; she ate fried chicken day after day with fried potatoes and sugared iced tea.

One day after visiting the doctor's office, May visited the house of Aunt Angie (Toby's first sister). Angie was glad to meet May; she was the nicest of all the aunts combined. She had made pumpkin pie for May to eat. She cut a slice of pie and topped it with ice cream, then she took a bite of pie. The fat content of pumpkin pie and ice cream and pie crust made her sick. Fried chicken and pumpkin pie had too many calories and she could not digest it good.

Three weeks after arriving in America, May gave birth to Otto, her first child. Without a husband standing by, giving birth was not easy. When she went into the hospital, Sue brought her lunch to eat. May was scared, but she knew she had to do it. And she talked to her unborn child; it was the moment she was waiting for since leaving home to travel to America. May's journey began with uncertainty. She said to the baby, "Okay, child, we are here and we can do this, and do your job, I cannot do it myself, and you have to help me, okay, child?"

At three o'clock, May had lunch with Sue, and then the doctor gave her a shot to speed up the childbirth. One or two hours went by; she was tired and slept. What they gave her made her sleepy. May could not stay awake. About an hour later, May saw Toby, then she saw that Toby was not in the room, and May saw Sue was there talking to her and trying to comfort her. May thought, *They must be taking turns watching over me, how lucky can I be?* Every contraction hurt, and she was tired. Then she talked again to her child for help, saying, "Please, please do your job, help me, I cannot do this myself."

She was so tired she slept; she was in and out for almost ten hours, and then the contractions got shorter and shorter. Next, May woke up when Sue went out in the hallway; she saw Toby come in, and then May fell asleep. May did not know how long she was asleep, but she felt uncomfortable; something did not feel good. Then she woke and felt something in her hand; Toby's warm, growing penis was in her hand. His hand was on top of hers, squeezing softly; Toby was looking at May and smiling. May pulled her hand free from Toby's hand as fast as she could. She did not know what to think; she shook like she had a nightmare.

May felt betrayed and assaulted by Toby; she had thought he wanted to have a fatherly relationship with her, like she would like to have, but at that moment, she was afraid, lost, and shocked. She wished for her husband to be there, but most of all she missed her own father; she remembered when she was only three years old, she went to Korea from Japan and asked for his help but was told he was no longer alive. May was asking, "Help me, help me, Dad. Please, Dad, be with me; let this monster go away."

She thought that she had found another dad, but Toby was a sexual pervert and predator. May felt dirty; she wiped her hand onto the sheet again and again. She cried silently and prayed that it was a bad dream and it would go away. She hugged her unborn child again and said to the child, "Please, you are going to be okay, and it was a horrible nightmare; you must not remember what happened tonight."

She was still tired and hurt by the contractions; a nurse stopped by to wake her, and she awoke with a flash about how the dirty old man came into her life. She wiped her hand onto the sheet again and again; she wiped her hand so many times, it looked like it had been bitten by a bug. May put her hand under the sheet, so that nurse could not see it. That day, Toby left a scar in May's heart and a deep hole in their relationship.

"It is going to be okay," she told herself. "Go back to sleep." Then she went back to sleep, calming down and trying not to cry. May went to sleep as long as she could, thinking that maybe the horrifying nightmare would go away. The child was as scared as the mother. The child was hanging onto the mother's cord; he wouldn't let go of it. Then the child came out with the mother's cord upside down; only his legs were showing. The doctor said she had to have a C section. After eighteen hours, May gave birth to her first child, but she did not want to go home with Toby and Sue.

The doctor explained to Toby and Sue, "May is petite, and the child was too big for her; she needs to recover from contractions." After May gave birth to Otto, she did not trust her husband's family. May did not talk to anyone except a counselor. Three months and three weeks later, Joe finally came home. May was glad to see him, but the trust was broken and she was inconsolable as to their future. May did not know how to solve this; she knew a long road was waiting for her. They lived a short time in Toby's house. Joe, May, and Otto's journey began; they went to Texas and never looked back. Notwithstanding, she did not talk about it until she had a gruesome nightmare many years later. May said to herself, "A virtual misunderstanding; stay calm, must be poised and balanced in my thoughts."

The moment that the trust was broken, the marriage was no longer with the husband and wife, it was to survive with the child. May's mental state was programmed in a short time, while she was in the hospital three months and three weeks before Joe came home from overseas. At that time, May surrendered to Toby's family with her child, Otto, his grandchild. May learned quickly to be a mother and not to show Toby and Sue and Joe that there was any danger. She maneuvered, planned, and controlled as she headed to the future.

CHAPTER 15
Who Is May?

May was born in Japan, and she went to her native Korea when she was three years old. She did not remember her father, only the shadow of his face. After they arrived in Korea, May's mom and dad divorced. Therefore, May thought her dad had passed away. She had one older brother (five years older) who was raised by Aunt Kim, her father's sister. Mother Kim did not talk about May's dad. May and her brother had no contact like brotherly love. Brother did stop by once in three years. One summer, her brother tried to teach her how to swim in a lake with a waterfall. Every weekend the children would hang out in that place. It was a beautiful place where a volcano had made a natural underground lake and a waterfall. The water was crystal clear and they wanted to jump in and swim.

Kim told her, "Hop onto my back, as I am going into the water. I am going to show you how to swim, okay, sis? As I swim, you are going to take a deep breath when I go into the water, and when I come out of the water, let go of your breath, okay, sis?" She did not understand what he was trying to say. Then he explained again. "Okay, sis, look at me and take breaths in and out. You do it, in and out." He was working hard to teach May how to swim. Shortly, she was on his back, into the water, and he was swimming to the other side of the lake. But she had a problem following her brother's instructions. She had problems breathing and thought she would drown.

Since that day, May did not see her brother again; it has been almost thirty years. But that day she had the sensation of drowning; she was also angry at her brother and could not forget. At the same time, her brother tried to help his little sister as a way of bonding. She missed him and wished to see him again, but it did not happen.

Five years after her divorce, May's mother married Mr. Lee, a high school principal. Kim was smart; she always had a business of her own. She found money whenever she needed it, from family or other resources. Mother Kim helped everyone in her family, including her male and female cousins. They worked as maids cleaning, cooking, and working in an office while they went to college.

Lee was smart; he could speak three different languages. He also had beautiful handwriting, and he loved to garden; he grew many flowers every year. May remembered that he had many exotic tropical plants like bananas and pineapples. One summer morning, the yellow flower of a cactus bloomed and popped open in front of May's eyes. She thought she could raise flowers just like her stepfather. Every summer, Lee made a rope out of hay and put a bamboo stick from the ground to the top of the roof, which was twenty feet wide and ten feet tall. The flowers bloomed in every corner of the back porch, and every morning in the summer, the blooms were luscious and lavish. It was a truly loveable, peaceful, and unruffled place that May always wanted to go back to. Every summer she would take a nap as she read many books.

During her childhood, she had many good memories; Lee was good natured in many ways, yet he did not take care of himself and died from heart disease. May began to grow into a young lady; at the same time, her cousin, who was six years older, was going to have an arranged marriage. She was beautiful, young, and appealing; she was a vegetarian. Overseas, when women reach sixteen to eighteen years old, their parents start looking for a man for their daughter to marry. In an arranged marriage, the parents must pick a man in the neighborhood with a degree of gravity, seriousness, and attraction. Rumors go out like lightning. When looking for a groom, they do not only go by his looks. Looks are important, but it is more important to know he can provide for his future bride.

Other issues include the following: He must be intellectually appealing and possess a high level of intelligence. He must have money in the bank. The looks come last. He must be acceptable in the parents' view. Finally, when the parents are satisfied, they pick a groom and introduce him to the bride-to-be. May knelt down and peeked through the living room door to see her cousin's groom. Her cousin was shy and withdrawn; she could not help but try to look at him out of the corner of her eye, with a tiny smile at the corner of her lip. At the same time, the groom-to-be tried to look at her; he was initially comforted and pleased; he was happy to see her. The meeting only took about forty-five minutes and was as beautiful as can be. May's mother set it up, and then her cousin went to the beauty shop. She was beautiful from head to toe, adorned and embellished. Her dress was made, the food was carefully cooked by the mothers and their maid. After five months, she got married. Their aunt who lived in Japan bought them a hotel. May's cousin had three boys of her own; she lived a good life. May missed her more than any of her cousins. She was like a sister, not a cousin.

After May's cousin got married and moved out, she was alone. Her mother thought it was a good idea to bring her cousin's brother to help with the house work. He was a handsome and smart young man, five years older than May. He helped with the house work and also worked in Kim and Lee's pawn shop. May went to an all girl's private school. She had to wear a starched uniform that was pressed with an iron. She was good at math and music. She wanted to be a singer, and she was the teacher's choice.

In Korea, on August 15, Independence Day, all students march in a parade to celebrate independence from Japan. All students voluntarily perform in public to commemorate the country. Parents liked to see their children march in the band, they are proud of them. It was a fun for May to go out in the street, playing drums with her friends. For two weeks every summer, she would learn how to be a lady, studying ethics, morals, principles, and structure that can help later in life. She did learn self-confidence and enthusiasm

The vegetarian monks taught May how to eat healthy food. She learned that nature gives us everything we need, we must take care of every living thing: trees and flowers and animals. Every summer on Arbor Day, everyone in the school would go to the mountains and plant evergreen trees. Evergreen trees were the Korean national tree and a symbol of long life. During the Korean War, bombs in the mountains destroyed almost 75 percent of the trees. The mountain was bare; for fifty-plus years, they planted evergreen trees, and now the bare mountain was green.

In Korea, mountains have many wildflowers, like roses, zinnia, and many others. One summer, May brought her stepfather, Lee, into the plant gate. Again, Lee put a bamboo stick between the front gate with a wire for the roses to climb. If the flowers tried to grow in another direction, he would redirect them to climb onto the bamboo climber. The sweet-smelling roses bloomed every year. There was an eight- to ten-foot-tall fence, and on top of the fence was broken glass. The roses climbed all the way to the top of the fence and started to bloom. The blooms at the top of the fence drooped down; it was as beautiful as can be.

In the summer, May visited her grandmother, uncles, aunts, and cousins. Kim had six siblings: four brothers and two sisters. Kim was the last child, and she helped her brothers and sisters. May enjoyed all the attention from her family, but most of all her visit with her grandmother was a special time she could not forget. May had pulled all the weeds growing in the mountain, collecting and drying them, making a scrapbook and putting everyone's names in it.

The most memorable year she had was when she was in seventh grade. Her sociology teacher wrote on the chalkboard, "Jealous envy." Then the teacher asked the students, "Do you know the meaning of jealous envy? What does jealous mean?"

No one's hand went up. All the students were dumfounded and looked at each other silently. The teacher began to explain, "Jealousy is not a good thing, the feeling comes from inside your heart and mind; if a person is better than you, jealousy kicks in and you want to do bad things to that person. There are many things that can be harmful to other people, like spreading rumors about something that person did or other lies. Sometimes, jealousy can cause physical, mental, and emotional pain. A jealous person has no respect, and a low-down person lies, cheats, steals, and kills." And then the teacher took a deep breath and asked, "Does anybody know how to solve the problems of jealousy?"

The students sat there looking at the teacher, dumfounded; they had no idea. Then the teacher began to give them directions of group exercises to educate themselves. At that moment, May learned self-reliance and how to be self-possessed. Most of all, she learned how to "live who you are, not somebody else."

As time went by, May's cousin was helping as much as he could; he cleaned and cooked. The food he cooked was good, and he helped May do her homework. Her mother was often away on businesses trips, and whenever Lee was out of state at business meetings, May was home alone with her cousin. She trusted him and talked to him like the brother she lost many years ago. He taught her many things her mom and dad could not teach her. She learned how to play twenty-one, the card game, and more. He showed that she could trust him and there was no harm. He played with May like he cared for her. But he was a bad boy.

May's mother had a pawn shop, where she loaned money to people and collected interest. One day she and Lee were gone for business. The customers stopped by the shop to pay interest. When a customer left the money, it was supposed to be put in the safety deposit box, but this day May's cousin did not put it there, instead, he put it in his pocket. May saw him do this, but could not believe that he was stealing the money. May confronted her cousin, who said, "Oh, I forgot to put it into the safety deposit box." He took the money out from his pocket and put it into the safety deposit box. May said to him, "Do not do it again, if I see you do it again, I will tell Mom and Dad!" Her cousin heard what she said, but soon he was doing it again. May wondered how to tell her mom and dad.

This zany buffoon of a young man had lived with the family for three years. One summer, after May marched with the band on Independence Day, she was hot and tired and just wanted to sit and drink cold water to cool down her body. She just wanted to lie down and take a nap. Her cousin knew that May's mother and stepfather would not be home. It was the perfect time for him to interact with May. He snuck into May's room and quickly pulled down his pants and lay on top of her. She woke up screaming, but he put his hand on top of her mouth and said, "Shhhh, be quiet, I am not going to hurt you." And then he raped her and said, "I lost my virginity to you and you lost your virginity to me, okay, sis?"

It was kooky, eccentric, and awkward; that bastard took her virginity by raping her. At that moment, May wondered, *Why?*

About six months later, May was only going through the motions;

she refused to accept the day-to-day moments. One day, she left of school on a Friday; and did not go home. She took a bus and rode as far as she could go. She did not tell anyone where she was going. She used every penny she saved from lunch money and babysitting, and she bought a ticket for as far as she could go. The next thing she knew, she was somewhere in the country with her school uniform and book bag.

When the bus stopped, one of the passengers looked at May and asked her, "Do know where you are going?"

She was so glad that someone had talked to her; it was a man and his wife. May started to cry and said, "I do not know where I am going; can you tell me where this place is?"

The couple could tell May was running from trouble. They said, "You must come with us."

She was so happy that the man and his wife invited her to their house in the countryside. They gave May a room to stay in and asked her to write a letter telling her mom and dad where she was.

May wrote to a friend, who took the letter to Kim. Kim was angry and went to get May; she brought two guards. As soon as May saw her mother, she tried to run from her. May did not know that there were guards on each corner; she could not go in any direction. Kim told May, "Time to go home; stop fighting me. What is the matter with you? Why are you doing this?" May tried to tell her mother what happened, but Kim would not listen to what May said. Instead, she told her, "Just be quiet and we'll talk when we get home." The train ride was almost ten hours long. When May went to the restroom, a guard stood by the door to make sure that she did not jump out. She was guarded every second. When the train stopped in their hometown, there was a taxi waiting. May sat between two guards all the way home. Then the taxi took them to an all-girls jail house.

May was mad and angry; she screamed at her mother, "Why do I have to stay here? I have done nothing wrong; tell me we are going home, Mom!" May was sobbing and said, "You do not know why I ran away from you? He raped me!" The guard heard what she said; he told Kim, "We think you need to hear what this young girl is trying to say to you."

Kim did not hear; she said to the guard, "She just wants attention, and she needs to take a lesson in discipline, that is all." Kim did not believe May. After one month in jail, May returned to school. She caught up on all the homework she missed, and she finished that year without any trouble. Gradually, Kim found out the boy was taking money from her, and she sent him back home where he should be. But this did not solve May's problem. May began to ignore her school projects and her grades fell. She wondered where her dad was; she had not seen him since she was three years old; she went places with her dad, but she did not know where they were going. Even so, the memory was vital. Every time she had a problem, she would always think her dad was with her, giving her a sense of comfort and hope. As she got older, she could not let go of the shadow of her father. May's high school graduation was coming up; her parents were looking to arrange a marriage for her. Kim was looking for a husband for May. But one day she had news from Aunt Kim, who called to say, "Father Kim passed away last night."

May did not know her father was living with another woman and had two daughters. It was like any other day; school was over and she was looking to see her friends and do their homework. Then her mother came into her room and sat quietly, holding her hand; May thought she was there to talk about the arranged marriage. She thought, *I am not ready to marry*, and she said, "Why are you being nice? Did you find my husband? I do not want an arranged marriage!"

She screamed in her mind to try to tell her mother that, but Kim said, "May, your father just passed away last night." "What are you talking about?" May asked. "Where did my father live? You did not tell me he was alive. I will not accept this arranged marriage, and forget the husband you are looking for!" May paused for five seconds, and then she got angry and said, "I am going to hate you forever! I want my dad! You do not understand how much I miss him and love him! Do you understand, Mom?"

It was unbearable to hear her father had been alive and she had two half sisters. She ran outside, slamming the door as hard as she could, and then she went to her friend's house. She did not come home until two days later. Kim and Lee knew she would be back.

May could not go to her father's funeral. It was the last time Kim talked to May about her father's death. Kim would not talk about what happened between she and May's father. May asked many times, but her answer always was, "It is in the past, I do not want to talk about it." That was the answer Kim gave May at that time. May had no answers from her mother as her life went along. She thought maybe one day she would tell her. May had to finish up high school. All that was going on in May's life could have kept her from finishing high school, but she did.

May fought against the arranged marriage, she did not want to marry that young, she wanted to explore the world if she could. She planned to stay with friends and go home once a month when she needed money. Three months went by, she knew that her best friend can be the best defense, but friends can also be your enemy. When you think you know your friend, then they become your enemy. May knew that she could not run from herself. May decided to face the facts and see the world. She believed that the only good was knowledge and the only evil ignorance, and she might trust others but she must keep her eye on herself. Even when you are asleep, you must your eyes open, your ears open, and your mouth closed. May thought, *The world is a dream, where I go, I see a dream, where I see, I see a dream.*

Thoughts:

Metamorphose into beautiful butterfly.

Beautiful butterfly grew with love and care.

As wings grew she learned to fly.

As she flew she became someone.

She flew over the mountain.

Flew over the sea. Flew across the bridge.

Nectar to nectar looking answer.

Evildoer a greeting with atrocity.

A greeting became hurtful, mournful.

Over the bridge tearful as sorrowful.

Broken wing, broken soul, and broken promise.

Time to sit down and adopt zest green tea.

Broken wing healed with zest green tea.

Broken soul begin to recover.

Teardrop becomes joyful as laughter.

Zest green tea become best friend.

Cup is float with zest green tea comfort.

Nothing is matter. And she flies again and again.

CHAPTER 16
Otto: Loved by Mom

It was a long journey with her son. Every parent has some kind of problem, so did May. Having a child is a joy, thinking about the future, to grow with love and hope. May's son did give her all that and more. She learned how to mother a child as well as to be a role model to her children. She also learned that with children, you have to give up some things to provide things for your children. She had to decide whether to work or go to college. She did not have in her mind that she had to get a job. The language barrier was hard. Many people come to America speaking another language, they think they will have a glamorous life, but the language barrier makes them the second choice, so they have to work harder. She had to give up things like clothes and shoes, among others. May tried to learn as many words as possible and carried a dictionary. Sometimes, people would try to help, but they often give you the wrong answer, and many people make a mistake on purpose, they laugh and spread rumors about how dumb you are.

May did not let them bother her; she did not put herself at their level. The judgment had to be May's; she had been taught by monks and teachers that life is only yourself, and you must watch your tongue. Try not to ask too many questions but listen to what others say, and don't make quick judgments about what is valuable to family and to children. With all that, children grow faster than you thought you saw yesterday. A child's life should have lessons and love from parents and grandparents. When Otto was three years old, his sister Kay was born. May would not allow Toby to visit without notice. Sometimes, Toby would invite May and Joe to his and Sue's house, saying, "We would like to see Otto and Kay."

May thought that was nice to hear and they would stop by their house. But they would find out that Toby did not want to see them, they were babysitting Lake's son and daughter, Junk and Cary, and they needed someone to play with them. May did not trust Toby around little girls. But she did not tell Joe what Toby had done to her when she was in the hospital giving birth. Toby knew what was going on himself, and he would tell other people, "Every time she passes in front of me, I feel ice water passing." He did not think May could hear what he was saying or understand what he was talking about, but she knew what he was saying. Toby should have been ashamed and conscious of his guilt, but he did not have any integrity.

Every time May and Joe visited while Toby was raising Lake's children, Cary would be sitting on his lap to play with Toby. May did not know at the time, and she thought that he loved Kay. One Christmas, all the family were visiting Toby and Sue to enjoy the holiday. Joe and May brought gifts and rushed to Toby's house. Otto was only three years old, and he loved to explore everything. He would examine, look at, inspect, and observe things, and he would sometimes get into trouble. But that's how young boys should be, not just sitting there doing nothing. Toby could not see the young boy's world. May thought, all boys should do some exploring; it helps a young boy to become a man.

That year, Christmas was eye catching to Joe; Otto sat under the Christmas tree, wondering what was in the presents wrapped in fancy paper, trying to touch them and investigate them, should he open the box, making inquiries as he sat there looking. May was helping Sue make dinner in the kitchen, and then they heard a child crying. Otto was only three years old and was crying for his mom. Toby was yelling at Otto, and with his big farmer's hands, he slapped Otto's tender face and yelled, "I told you not to touch anything! Stop it!"

May looked out of the corner of her eye and saw Toby's hand slapping Otto's tender face. Most of all she was shocked. Then May scooped Otto into her arms and took him into the other room. Otto's cheek was red and he could not stop crying. That moment she had to hug Otto and tell him she loved him. She wiped his cheek with a tender hand and hugged him, saying, "I love you, son, I love you. Stop crying, it is going to be okay, and Mom loves you, okay?"

Otto stopped crying and hugged her, saying, "I love you too, Mom."

"Now, when we go back to the living room, do not touch anything, okay, son?"

"Okay, Mom," he said and hugged his mom; he understood that when they went out to the living room, he must not touch anything unless someone gave him a gift and his mother told him to open it.

That year, she wanted to get out of that family, but she did not know how to. The following year, May had a little girl. At the same time, Joe lost his job and was looking for a new job. It was the perfect time to get away from Toby. When she came to America, she brought her own money and had enough for a down payment for a house, and they bought a house. Two year later, the house they bought gave them credit to buy the next house, and they moved away from Toby's hometown.

Moving away from a small town to a city scared Joe, but to May it was an adventure, it did not scare her. She grew to love the city, and it gave her more courage. The day after Thanksgiving, they packed and moved into their new home, feeling good as can be. Kay was ten months old and Otto was almost five. As they were driving to their new home, the kids did not know where they were going, they only knew they were going home.

Joe had a new job and unpacked all the dishes and clothes; they ate their first meal without a phone call from Toby, asking what they were eating. The children slept good, and the next day he started his new job. May thought, *This is going to be okay now, and the future will begin with Joe, Otto, and Kay.* Soon, Otto had to go to school. He was excited and met new friends. Sometimes, boys and girls wanted to play with Otto and Kay. It was nice to know that someone cared, and they appreciated living in a friendly environment; they showed gratitude and thankfulness.

In his first three years at school, Otto got good grades. In fourth grade, he wrote a letter for Mother's Day. His teacher thought it was good enough to enter in a contest in the community newspaper. What he wrote was very simple: "I love my mother, because she helps me with my homework, she cooks for me, and she loves me and my sister. I love my mother more than anything in the world."

May was humbled by the letter; she wanted to love her children and tried to help them in any way she could. But one day, Otto came home and went straight into his room, shutting the door without saying hello to his mom or kissing her cheek. May knew something was wrong. She fixed him some milk and cookies, went down the hallway, and knocked on the door, asking, "Hi son, where is my hug? I brought milk to drink with your favorite cookies!"

He did not respond. May was beginning to panic. Something was wrong with him. She said, "I am going to come in, okay, son?"

She opened the door gently and saw Otto was crying; he had crawled into the corner of the bed, trying not to see his mother. A mother knows when her child has a problem. May carefully sat beside him and asked again, "What is the matter, son, why are you crying? Talk to me."

He did not want to talk about school; maybe he had a fight with some boys. Seeing Otto cry made May's heart pound, and her mind was spinning. Again she said, "Please talk to me, son, I love you, when you cry, I am going to cry and it hurts me too. Please talk to me."

She thought that he must have had a fight with some boys, so it should not be a big deal. Then he cried again and choked up; what had happened hurt him deeply. May thought quickly, *Your tongue is your ambassador*. And she carefully hugged Otto and said, "It is okay to cry, but you must tell me what happened today, stop crying and talk to me. If you do not tell me, then I will not know what you are crying about, son, please tell me." She sat beside him and told him how much she cared for him and loved him, saying that he could talk to her and trust her.

He became calm and stopped crying; he said, "One kid spit in my face and said to me, 'Go home where you came from, dumb Chinese boy.'"

When May heard this, she said, "I am so sorry. First, you are not a Chinese boy; you are Korean, and you are a young, smart, handsome man."

Otto was emotionally hurt, embarrassed, flustered, and confused. He was choked up and overly affected. Seeing him cry made May madder; she wanted to grab that other child and spank him. May and Otto's pride was hurt, and she wished to tell all parents to teach their children with an open mind. Otto knew Mom was mad and he needed to stop crying.

May regained her composure and tried to explain things to him, saying, "People who bully others are not good; most of the time they have no education and they do not know right from wrong. Those people are dopes, dweebs, and imbeciles. They are dumbbells."

May was careful to encourage and educate Otto. Sometimes, it is okay to cry and hurt, but we should learn from our mistakes, and hurting people is a bad thing; we should not hurt other people. Otto was eager to learn what his mother had to say. "Sometimes, children are bullies; they are hateful, obnoxious, and loathsome to other children, but you must not forget all that we have talked about today, okay, son? I love you, son, and I am always with you. If you do not understand, then I will listen any time; do not forget."

May hugged him again, and Otto gave his mom a hug and said, "I love you, Mom, and I will not forget what you taught me today." Kind words can be short and easy to speak, but their echoes are truly endless, May thought. And Otto had courage, grace under pressure; he understood that he should not bully others. Otto was good to his sister and to his friends. And he was good at school and listened to his mother, and he gladly respected his mother.

He was engaged in many school activities, with football, orchestra, and band, playing violin in school concerts and on many holidays. Any mother would be proud of this son and daughter. May proudly talked about Otto and Kay. Where was Joe while all these things were going on? When you have children, both parents should be involved with their care and love. But Joe was not there for his children 99 percent of his time; he was not there to help with their homework, play football with Otto, or do other things. What was his excuse? His job. Everyone had a job, that was no excuse. As adults, mothers and fathers should stand beside their principles and help their children to grow. Joe was working as a truck driver, but the one job he had did not provide enough income. May had to go to work, and she did not know what kind of job she could get. May had no experience and no skill or job training. With that, who would help the children with their homework, May wondered.

Meanwhile, she would help the children do their homework in the kitchen, including doing the math that she learned when she was young. May knew math skills were extremely important, so she passed on the math skills she learned from schools. May had the children practice and do their homework for one hour after school; they worked fast and accurately. As they did their homework, they took time out for milk and cookies, and then practiced more math before they could go out and play with their friends. One day while they were doing so, Joe was looking over May's shoulder and said, "I would like to practice math with the kids. Can I?"

May did not believe what she heard; it made her lost and in denial; she asked, "What did you say? Repeat that again, please?"

"I do not know how to do simple math!"

"You say what? How did you graduate high school?"

"Back then, everyone could graduate just by reading a little English."

She did not want to inflame him with questions in front of the children. She acted like nothing was the matter until that night, and then she said, "You were not an honest person, you should have told me before you married me." She paused a minute.

He started to cry and hug May, but she shoved him away and asked again, "What happened to you? Didn't you go to school?"

He started crying again and told May what happened with Toby and with school. Joe had a problem because Toby wanted to have another girl but he was born instead. Toby did not want to have him around and he did not learn what he needed to learn from his father.

May was shocked and angry; she wondered what she could do now, she had to make a choice soon: stay with this family and help it grow or get out of it, thinking of herself, and go back home. If May went back home, what would happen to the children she loved more than anything in the world? She had lost her trust, and it would take a long time to gain trust back, if ever.

May realized that she had a long road to get where she was going. Many nights, she cried in bed by herself, trying to hold some kind of hope in her heart. There was always hope. May thought that giving up her children was a failure. She could not allow Toby to take care of Otto and Kay. If May did that, then it would break her heart. Her voice was strong, and failure was not an option. But she knew she did not have any feeling for Joe; the trust was gone forever.

She thought and thought for many nights by herself, and then she said to Joe, "I am going to stay with you and my children and raise Otto and Kay; after all, we brought them into this world and must be responsible parents, then I will determine where we are going." After pausing for a second, she said, "The children are more important for right now, and I need you to work with the children; please pay attention to the kids, do not ignore them."

At the same time, she told him what happened during Otto's birth when he was not there, including the sexual assault by Toby, and therefore, there was no trust. As Joe listened, he sat quietly. May realized by Joe's reaction that he did not want to be around the children. All the same, she was doing a father's job, playing sports with Otto; his father should have been playing football or basketball with him. At the same time, May had to go to work, so the children would have a roof over their head and food on the table.

Otto grew into a smart young man, in one year he could have a car and drive to school. May was looking forward to seeing him drive. On the weekends, children from the neighborhood came over to May's backyard and played with Otto and Kay. They played hide-and-seek and caught lightning bugs. Otto often played commanding soldier. He nailed plywood into a big maple tree and built a tree house and made steps to climb into it. The boys and girls had fun almost every week. Sometimes, the neighbors would bring their children, thinking that May would babysit, and they would go out shopping; they often did not come back for five hours.

One afternoon in the fall, it was beautiful; the colors were changing: yellow, red, and so on. It was in October, close to Otto's birthday. All the leaves covered the backyard. Many children were playing in the leaves that were raked up to clear the yard. May roasted apples and marshmallows and hot dogs. She had planted two apple trees in the backyard; they were big and beautiful, and every year they bloomed with apples. The children liked roasted apples; they would come around asking for more. May always had some for them to eat. She also had dry fish, because she thought they should eat more seafood. The friends were curious, and they liked to taste salty sweet dry fish and asked for more. May wanted her children to make friends and learn leadership and fellowship.

One day, Otto came home from school and went out to play in the leaves and help rake them. May thanked him for helping and said, "Okay, son, I love you for helping." May cooked Otto's favorite dinner, which was fried chicken. Around six o'clock, she called to Otto, "Son, dinner is ready! Time to eat; come in!" She called from kitchen door, thinking he was going to come in; usually he would hear his mother, come into the kitchen, and sit at the dining table beside her, but today it did not happen.

When he came in from outside, he said, "I do not feel like eating; I am going to do my homework, okay, Mom?"

May thought nothing was the matter, he just wanted to do his homework, so she let him go to his room. She was not worried that he did not eat, because the doctor had told her not to push her children to eat; and when they are hungry, they will let you know. But she had an empty feeling, like the chair he sat on in the corner was empty. She tried again and said, "I fixed your favorite dinner, fried chicken with mashed potatoes!"

"I am not hungry, okay, Mom?"

"Okay, son, do your homework."

It was a mistake to let him go and not check what was the matter. The next day, his boss called from where Otto was working after school, saying she needed to come right away to pick him up. May did not feel good that his boss called one hour early. Something was wrong. May rushed to his work place, and he was waiting for her to pick him up.

When May saw Otto, she asked, "Are you okay, son?"

Then he showed his mother his leg and ankle; May could not stop herself and threw up; at the same time, she went to the drugstore to ask for help. Otto went into the pharmacy; he unwrapped his ankle and showed the pharmacist. The skin was peeling with medicated tape. It was red and swollen, and the skin was stuck to the tape; it was oozing.

The pharmacist saw Otto's leg and said to May, "This child needs to go to the emergency room."

May was crying and asked Otto what happened to his ankle;

how could he go to school and then go to work? May could not yell; she tried to calm down, but she could not look at him. If she looked at him, she might scream her lungs out. May's nerves were shaking, and she had to push back her dinner with her tongue so she wouldn't throw up again.

She drove as fast as she could to the hospital. There were many other sick people waiting in the ER who needed attention, so they had to wait as one person went in and wait as another person went out. They kept hoping they were next; sitting with all the sick people, it seemed like they waited longer than she waited to give birth. Finally, the ER doctor saw Otto and diagnosed him with third-degree burns on his ankle and leg.

When they left the ER, Otto knew he needed to tell his mother what happened. He hugged her and said he was sorry for all that trouble.

May said, "Son, I love you, and I am glad you are alive and did not get hurt more than you were; it could have been worse, and I accept your apology. But you have to explain what happened last night. And this is not the first time you played with fire, it is the second time, do you know that?"

"I do not remember; what was the first time I played with fire?"

"Just tell me what happened last night."

"Okay, Mom, I thought I would burn the leaves after I raked them, and I took lawnmower gasoline and poured it onto the leaves, then the wind carried the gasoline onto my legs; I was not thinking, and I lit the leaves and the wind carried the flames onto my legs, and the fire would not stop. I tried to put it out with the rake, and my leg and shoes were burned." He cried to his mom.

May said to Otto, "Stop crying. I love you, and the most important thing is that you are alive; it could have been much worse, and you are going to be okay." May comforted Otto and asked how he made it through the night and went to school.

"Well, I could not sleep, so I took three aspirin, and I slept good last night, but this morning I took a shower and it hurt, so I took three more aspirin and went to school. Then, when I went to work, I showed my boss, and he called you."

"Why didn't you tell me last night?"

"I was scared to tell you, Mom."

"You should never ever be scared to tell me again; if you do not tell me, I am going to be madder—do you understand, son?"

"Okay, Mom, I will not play with fire again, and I will tell you, okay, Mom?" Then he asked, "What happened the first time? I do not remember; can you explain, Mom?"

May recalled this memory: "I do not think you remember our first house, but in our second house, about three weeks after your sister, Kay, came home from the hospital, I was giving her a bath. You usually stood by me watching, and when I was ready to dry her off, you would hand me a towel, but one day you were not there. I wondered where you were, because you were there a minute ago, and I said to myself, *I need to check on that boy.* I wrapped Kay with a towel and held her in my arms; I walked into the kitchen, calling your name, but you did not answer. At that point, I was worried when I did not see you; I turned the corner, and you were sitting on the floor next to the wall, lighting a fire. If I had not caught it at that moment, there could have been a fire and we would not have had a place to stay; the house would have been gone, and we would have been in the street. That was the first time you played with fire."

He sat quietly and asked again, "How old was I?"

"You were only three years and six months, and I was not mad about that—I love you too much to be mad—but you must not play with fire again, okay, son?"

May took Otto out to show him how to drive, trying to be a father; she replaced Joe's action since he no longer acted like a father to Otto. It was a good lesson for mother and son, and they had fun.

Otto learned how to drive straight off, immediately, at once, without delay. After May taught him how to drive, she thought that now she could finish college and become an accountant; it would take her two years to earn a degree. As soon as he passed the driver test, May thought he should have a fast and sporty car to drive. Joe and May saved every cent and bought him a Ford Mustang. It was a big mistake; all his friends wanted to ride with him. He became the center of attention and a bad boy. He started to show off and hang out with other young men. These boys had no hope and were neglected by their parents; they were sixteen years old with a drinking problem and so on. He was blindsided by the liability and exposure of these so-called friends. May was alarmed that these delinquents were coming into his life in a short time.

One day, he invited a friend to spend the night without letting May know. The next morning, Otto did not come out to eat breakfast. May thought again that she needed to check on him. She saw the other boy sleeping in Otto's room.

May asked Otto, "Why is this boy in your room?"

He answered, "Can he live with us? He does not have a place to stay; his mom kicked him out. Please, can he stay with us?"

"No son, the problem he has with his mom is not my problem, he needs to go home and talk with his mom, and you tell him he has to go!"

May did not like the friends Otto was hanging out with; they were drinking and doing drugs, and they had girlfriends. At that time, Otto had the chance to work in a lumber yard. Otto was curious and eager to learn, and he tried everything in his power. That spring, flowers were blooming, and growing plants in the yard gave May a sense of hope. It was May's favorite season, and she always grew flowers and other plants. She used to see Lee do this every year and learned from him what to do.

Otto knew his mom liked growing things, and he brought home some herbal plants. He wanted to grow them in his closet. He bought a light for the plants and learned how to water them. May had no idea what was going on in his room. She was thinking that he was going to be okay. One day she came home from work and went to his room to check on how the herbal plants were doing. In a sense, she was spying on him, but every parent should pay attention to what is going on with their children. May did not regret snooping on him.

She opened the closet door; his herbal plant had grown big; it looked like it would take over the closet soon. May wondered what kind of herb it was. She knew a lot about flowers and herbs, but she had never seen herbs grown in a closet. That day, Joe was home early from work; she took him into Otto's room and asked, "What is this? I do not usually see plants growing in a closet. Can you tell me?"

As soon as Joe saw the plant, he started shaking and screamed, "This is not a plant; this is a drug that people smoke!" It was marijuana.

May had no experience farming, growing plants, or working in a greenhouse. She only knew what her stepfather did with flowers. Joe explained, "If you are caught growing this drug in the house, you will be sent to jail—do you understand, May? Because I do understand; now how are we going to solve this problem?"

They had to think fast before Otto came home. They looked all over the place for something to use to kill that plant. They had to be careful about what kind of chemical they used so he did not know. They thought quickly and decided to use rubbing alcohol, which evaporates into the air quickly and leaves no smell. They both thought it was a good idea, and they poured some onto the plant every day. In two weeks time, the plant began to die; the leaves dropped off, and the stem became hollow. The plant was not going to make it. Joe and May avoided eye contact at the dinner table so they would not let Otto know what they were doing. It took three weeks to kill the plant.

One day, Otto came home and ran into his room to look at the plant; he wondered why the plant was dying, and then he came out and said, "Mom, the herbal plant I planted is dying; I am going to put it out in the garden."

"Okay, son, I am sorry the plant did not make it; maybe another time."

She smiled at her success in killing the illegal plant. She knew that he could grow it again in the future, but who says raising children is easy? Having a child means to hope in the future, learn how to love, and more. Teaching and helping them to grow says to the children, "Be honest, and do not steal; if you get in trouble, do not lie." May learned from school and her parents that being honest is the best way to live. She raised her children and gave them that wisdom, teaching them to apply those rules to their years. May did not ever tell Otto about the plant, and now is the time for him to learn what she did; she has no regrets.

CHAPTER 17
Infatuated: Marrying and Moving Out

An empty stomach is not a good political adviser; May is all about education. She grew up overseas, all about education. May's mission was to send her children to the university. When Otto was nineteen years old, he went to university. It was the first time he lived away from home, with no help from Mom and Dad. Joe was not much help, but he was there as something.

Otto had a girlfriend; she was two years younger than him. He was helping her with math homework, and she became his girlfriend, and then she became his wife. G. Hock had a child. When she was nine years old, her father raped her. He should have been put in jail, but her mother did not want him to go to jail, and she bailed him out. Miss Hock learned to not trust any women. Miss Hock became a rebellious child. She began drinking when she was nine, doing drugs and skipping school. With her charm, blonde hair, and slender build, no one noticed. Otto did not know he was falling in love with her. But her mission was to pay back every man she met. While Otto and Hock were dating, they would argue about who did what; they had a problem with trust. Otto could not accept her behavior; it was like a story about witches. He was taught by his mother to never hit a woman. If you are in danger by that woman, you must walk away from her;

do not argue and do not ever hit a woman. He heard this many times from his mother.

One day after he came home from work, G. Hock called Otto. She needed help, explaining, "There was black man and he tried to stop my car and get in it and ask for money, but I fought and got away from him. Please help me."

Otto was baffled and frustrated about what to do; he picked her up and took her home, helped her, comforted her, and spent the night at her house. This is what she wanted, and her wish came true. Another time, Otto was working in a parking lot. When he finished work and was ready to come home, he walked out to the parking lot, and there was G. Hock, beside her car, which had a broken back window. She was crying, "Help me, help me, some man tried to rob me; he broke my window to get into my car, please help me, Otto, I love you, Otto, please help me."

He could not believe that a man was there to hurt her. When he saw the broken window, all the glass was in the backseat; if a man was trying to break in her car, then the glass should have been outside in the parking lot. That just made common sense. But G. Hock told Otto that all her actions were because she loved him and wanted to have him, to please him, and to pay attention to him. "Please, who is she trying to fool? Not me."

May laughed and told Otto, "Do not forget, we have talked about putting hands onto a woman; do not ever hit a woman." He understood clearly and he followed the directions his mother taught him, that hitting a woman is not an option. That year he went back to the university for his second year. At the same time, she went to the local college and got a two-year degree as a dental assistant. Otto did not tell his mother he was dating her. But G. Hock could not leave him alone. She begged and begged him to come home to finish school; she said she loved him.

One day, Otto called Mom to say he could not stay in university, because his grades were dropping and he had to drop out. May was perplexed, and they had a long talk. "Son, what happened at university is passed; now, if you do not want to go to university, then you must go to the local college and get a two-year degree. You do not have a choice or option, you have to do it."

He cried and asked May, "Why do I have to go to local college?"

"If you do not have an education, how are you going to get a job with good pay? How are you going to raise your family? Don't you want to get married?"

"Yes, I do want to get married and have a child!"

"Then you must have some education. I am going to let you stay rent free in your room; you do not have to pay any rent money. Many parents ask for money for room and food and many things; you can live here free, but you have to save money yourself, and you must finish the degree in two years. It can help you get a job, a good-paying job—do you understand, son? And you can get more education if you want to, which many people do."

At the same time, May wanted to ask him if he was dating Miss Hock, but she did not want to push. When he was twenty-one years old, he got a degree in accounting and was hired as an assistant accountant. He was the youngest accountant ever hired by that company, and he had a good job in a good corporation. He could advance far with his abilities; Otto had great abilities in math.

At the same time, Miss Hock was seeing him and providing him with drugs and alcohol.

After Otto graduated, May bought him suits, shoes, and ties, to fit into that corporation. May came from a business family and knew you had to always be planning—it is the prelude to success. She would have liked to finish a degree herself, but she did not have the time and energy to do it, because she had to be both mother and father and earn an income to put food on the table. She still hoped to do this. Then she realized that Otto was talking about marrying this girl, who was lying and cheating him. May had no choice; she had to accept that he wanted to marry Miss Hock. Otto could not see what love was and did not see that she was using him.

Otto had saved some money living rent free; he did not have to buy food or clothes. Miss Hock finished school in two years; she earned a degree and got a job in a doctor's office. Both she and Otto were working, and they had good-paying jobs. They were engaged in a matter of months and set the wedding date for the same week as May's birthday. Miss Hock's parents liked Otto as their future son-in-law, and they gave them a down payment for their house. May got along with Otto's future bride. The wedding day was beautiful. There was a big church with a crowd of people who knew the family. The bride's mother weighed over four hundred pounds; she had surgery to lose weight, but it did not make much difference with her looks. At the reception, there were gifts in the hallway, and the table was overflowing with gift boxes. It could have been in a larger room, people showed up unexpectedly with thoughtful gifts. It pleased by both parents and their families and friends.

But May was sad; she could not be happy on Otto's wedding day. She was looking forward to the last dance with her son, but Miss Hock's friends would not let her get close to Otto. Every time she tried, there was Miss Hock, or her mom, or her dad (a child molester who should have been in jail), looking at May. May did not have a chance to dance with Otto, whom she loved more than her life.

Miss Hock's mother was as drunk as her daughter. They could not walk straight, their speech was slurred, and they made a scene on the wedding day. Both daughter and mother were drunk as goats; the father grabbed his daughter and danced, acting like nothing was the matter. At the end of the reception, Toby left with flowers without bothering to ask May; the wedding flowers should have been given to someone else, not the feisty, ill-behaved Toby. Otto's life was moving on. May did not have the chance to tell him, and she wanted to tell him that he had graduated and was getting married and she loved Miss Hock like a daughter, that she wished them both a happy life. May felt sorry that she could not tell them. What was going to be next? May and Joe were invited to Hock and Otto's first Thanksgiving dinner at their new house. They were excited because they would be able to tell Miss Hock, "We love her as a daughter."

May and Joe rushed to Otto's home. They knocked on the door, but it took a long time to answer. Okay, May thought, newlyweds were sleeping late.

Soon the door opened; Otto looked at May and screamed in her face, "You guys are too early!" He was yelling and his voice was harsh and rough. Otto's eyes were rolling, and he walked into the kitchen to have some coffee.

May did not think they would enjoy their first Thanksgiving dinner at Otto's home. It was a proud moment for May, and it was long journey with Otto; May was looking forward to seeing that he had a nice home. Every parent wants to see their child marry and have a dream home and begin their future; they look forward to having grandchildren. When Hock came downstairs, she did not say one word, she just tried to light the fireplace. As she lit the fireplace, the wind was blowing into the chimney, causing smoke to go in the living room.

Otto did not like way she lit the fireplace and yelled, "How many times do I have to tell you, do not light the fireplace when it's a windy day!" He put out the fire and sat beside his father to drink coffee. May saw something was wrong again. Otto's actions, movements, and body language were telling May that something was wrong.

May had never seen him this mad, and he knew never to yell loudly at a woman or put his hands on one. That day what May saw was not him. May was irritated and thought they had intentionally set it up to deliberately argue with her. Hock began talking about an issue she had a problem in the past when dating Otto two years earlier. She asked May, "Why did you tell Otto that he did not love me? Otto, why didn't you dance with your mom at the wedding?" May and Joe were lost; they were shocked and could not make sense out of her. What was the point of bringing up the past? It was not true that May did not tell Otto she loved him. May did not tell anyone about not dancing with Otto on his wedding day; how did she know?

May tried not to be a thorny mother-in-law that was not easy to please. Hock was going on and on, "Why did you not stop by more often? And why did you not tell your son you love him?"

Every time she spoke, May tried to explain to Otto, but she was cut down and could not speak to him.

May told Joe, "Take her outside. I need to talk to him one-on-one; after that, I will talk to you!" She was out about five seconds and pushed Joe into the wall before leaving the kitchen. Joe started to get annoyed and bothered and told her, "You need to let go of your anger!"

Hock and Joe went out the door. May tried to calm down and carefully talk about an extremely touchy subject; as calm as she could be, she said to Otto, "I love your wife, and we are glad that you two are married, and you know I love you more than anything. I did not come around every week because you two are newlyweds. We thought you should have space with your wife; you do not want me to come around every week, do you?" Otto was weeping and not saying anything. May said to him again,

"We love your wife like our daughter, do you understand that? And we are very happy with your marriage!"

He began to calm down. At the same time, he said, "Mom, if you did not help me, I could not have finished school, could not have gotten a good-paying job and marry her, as well as the house that I have right now. I am so grateful for all that. And I love you to love my wife."

She gave him a hug and said she loved him again and again. Then they needed to talk to Hock. Otto went upstairs, weeping. As Hock came in from outside, she saw where he was and tried to sit on the kitchen chair; she could not sit on the chair and almost fell on the floor.

May helped her up and calmed her down. Hock opened the dialog with May, asking, "Why did you not tell your son you love him?" May had no idea what she was asking; throughout Otto and May's journey, for twenty-three years, she always told her son she loved him. May looked at her and shook her head, lost; she did not know how to answer and explain. She tried to argue, and her voice began to rise as she said to May, "Yes, I had sex with your son two years ago, and you did not like it!"

When May heard this, her voice wanted to hurt her. May remembered one day two years ago that, when she came home from work, she did not hear her son or daughter in the house. The house was very quiet; May walked down the hallway and opened the door to Otto's room. Otto had no clothes on and lay in the bed. Miss Hock was in her underwear and already on top of him. They knew May was in the house; they heard her footsteps all the way to Otto's room. Hock was planning to show May she was a bad girl.

May had to tell him, "She needs to go home. And don't do it again in my house; don't show me you and your girlfriend having sex."

May was insulted, and her pride was degraded; the damage was done, and she had lost trust in her son.

As she left, Otto asked May, "Can Hock live with us?"

"No, son, she cannot."

He explained, "She has a problem with her mom and dad, because her dad raped her and her mom did not believe in her. She does not get along with her dad; please, Mom!"

May knew that Miss Hock needed to talk with her mom, not May, and she said to Otto, "Son, that is a big problem; she has to talk with her parents. I cannot let her live here, and that is final!" Miss Hock was raped by her dad, and then she was raping Otto as retaliation and revenge to every man she met. May firmly let Otto know that the answer she was looking for was not Otto or May. After their talk, she did not think it was her business, and she thought Miss Hock had talked with her parents.

When Miss Hock said that May did not believe her, she told her, "Whatever happened with your dad, I cannot solve that problem for you; you have to talk with your own parents, not with me. I do believe what you are saying; please calm down, dear, and we do love you like our own daughter, dear!"

May tried to explain that she had been hurt by her mother and father; she should have been loved and given attention by her family. She was acting like a little girl, but she could not control her motive for saying May was a bad mother-in-law. She made a fuss and complained vigorously, and then she looked upstairs at Otto and become like a mad dog, foaming at the mouth; she screamed, "Otto, tell your mom you love me right now!"

Otto heard and said out loud, "I love you, Hock!" He was weeping and sitting on the stairs.

This happened four months after the wedding. May could not

take Otto crying and looking like a lost puppy, but she knew not to get involved with newlyweds; if not, it can cause more problems in the marriage. When you cannot see the son you love dearly and have been with for twenty-three years, it was hard to let go of it. For all that, every mother wishes that there is hope.

Otto worked in an office not too far from May's home. She thought she might stop by to see him and say hello or have lunch with him; she drove by the office and glanced over, hoping to see him, but then she just drove away. Then one day, May was driving around, and Otto was going to lunch; he realized his mom's car was behind him. He was scared to talk to her and drove away at high speed. Otto ran away from his mother. May could not stop Otto, and she let go of him with love and hoping he would do well.

After they were married for three years, all her lies and drinking and doing drugs caught up with Miss Hock. As soon as she married Otto, she told him, "I have been an alcoholic since I was nine years old, and I have cheated on you, too."

Otto could not believe it; he thought that he loved her and forgave her and loved her more. Hock told him the truth about her past. Otto knew about all that, but he thought he loved her and let her tell him. She became alarmingly inebriated and more alcoholic. She started to go to work drunk, and at lunch she would drink booze. When she came home, she would be inebriated at dinnertime. They began arguing; she said he loved his mom more than her, and this went on nonstop for almost three years.

Otto had no choice; he sent her to alcohol rehab. The money they had saved and a second mortgage were nothing compared to her recovery, which was priceless. She came home in one month but then relapsed; still, he did not give up and tried to help her again. Otto saw he had to let go of her as soon as he could.

May knew that Miss Hock was obnoxious, vile, hostile, and

hateful. It could have been avoided. But for Otto, the truth was an unpopular subject, because it is unquestionably true, and she was characterized by hardships with her parents that she needed to confront herself.

May knew Miss Hock must face the truth and confront her dad; her only hope was to get help. Otto learned a life lesson. He was dim-witted and in puppy-love; his infatuation continued through five years of marriage. May saw Otto's life crumbling with an alcoholic with his new friends. Being single and having a house and good-paying job did give him chance to go out visiting other people. At the same time, he needed a man he could trust to lead him where he wanted to go, not Mom. Otto craved attention from his father, but Joe could not give it to Otto. Rather, May tried to give Otto attention, but he began to rebel against women, and he became defiant and mutinous.

Trust is earned by many, but without impairment, Otto had a disadvantage. Indeed, every time he visited Toby, his grandfather had showed him how to act toward women; he had a nasty personality that was hopeless, obnoxious, crude, and cranky; he was an unpleasant man. Otto saw this and started acting like Toby. Young, handsome, and smart, Otto began to confuse and mystify; Joe could not show him how to act; instead, Otto ignored him. May did all the stress; it was not Joe's job to give Otto attention.

May watched as Otto, the love of her life, paid the casualty in a bad marriage to Miss Hock; her sacrifices became failure, it was a wasted investment. Otto was lonely and deprived, he began to drink and make the wrong friends; all his mother could do was let time come; he would marry again and be a good man and husband and father that the family can count on. May has always stressed education to Otto. And May stands by that. At the same time, you cannot find the truth where you are; where else do you expect to find it? You must ask yourself where you are and where you are going.

To the son I dearly love:

Open eyes wide to see clearly.

Smell with nose before to test if rotten.

Hear with ear wisdom to thought.

Watch open mouth slanderous tongue-lashing.

Good, bad, and ugly. With them in all.

CHAPTER 18
Loving Daughter

Having a daughter brought May joy as well as happiness. Kay was born with blonde, curly hair that made May and Joe gleeful. The family was very happy and always wanted to see her, and Toby often invited them to visit his house. When Kay was nine months old, May and Joe moved to city, where they lived for thirty years. May loved her son and daughter equally. Often overseas, the son is more important because he will take care of Mom and Dad and the family heritage will be passed on to him. But May did not believe this, which she thought was from the old Stone Age. May had an open mind; she remembered history learned from school; from her stepfather, Lee; from her mother, Kim; and from the monks. May thought with all the family values, she would live in the new world and show respect to her daughter as well as to her son, giving them equal attention. The master does not take sides and must give the children equal attention no matter what.

Kay grew and was ready to start kindergarten. May loved her little girl, Kay. She was the icon of the family and attracted attention everywhere she went. Kay was a frisky, playful, lively young girl; everyone loved her. Kay's journey began with kindergarten. She came back from school on the first week, crying to May, "Mom,

I had to stand in the corner of the classroom by myself because I cannot skip. Mom, can you teach me how to skip?"

When May heard this, she got angry at the teacher; if a young child cannot skip, she should not be degraded by standing in the corner of the classroom. Kay was not a dancer, and she did not come from Hollywood being pushed by her parents. It was another way to use a child to show one's ego. May decided to help her; that day, they were in the kitchen and she showed Kay how to skip. She said, "Okay, Kay, you do like I do: your left foot goes up at the same time your right foot hops, and then your left foot comes down and right foot goes up, okay, dear?"

Kay learned how to skip quickly and gracefully; this made her self-confidence as high as it could be.

Twenty-five years later, May, Otto, and Kay gave their time in community service, packing bags of food for people in need. Meeting new friends and donating time is a good thing, and they did this whenever they had the time to do so. Giving time to the community is a beautiful feeling. Kay loved to help and so did Otto.

Young boys and girls liked to be around Kay, and they liked play with her and talk to her. Kay made friends with a third grade boy and asked him, "Do you know how to skip?"

The young boy told Kay, "No, I do not know how to skip; can you show me?"

Kay showed that young boy how to skip. May was as proud as can be; she loved helping other children. Great work is performed not by strength but by perseverance.

While Kay was in first and second grade, May went back to college to finish her education. She was going to college to become an accountant. She believed that schooling would increase her chance of survival. Whenever May had the chance, she did not stop learning. One day, May came home early and was doing her homework. Soon, Kay came home from school; she liked to get attention from her mom, but May just said hello to Kay while she did her homework. She did not ask Kay how her day was at school. Usually, May welcomed Kay after school and gave her a snack to eat and milk to drink. That day, she had too much homework; May did not give Kay attention and continued to do her homework. Not saying hi and not paying attention to Kay was a mistake.

Kay got mad and said, "Mom, I am home, Mom!"

May heard and realized she had not paid attention to her daughter; she said to Kay, "Oh no, I am so sorry, dear. I had to finish this homework. I will get you cookies and milk, okay, dear? We can do our homework together."

Kay did not like May's answer. Kay needed a hug and a smile on May's face. But Kay had a cold feeling about her mom. After a short moment, she grabbed a kitchen knife and pointed it at May's nose, saying, "I want you to die!"

She yelled at May again and again. May could not believe what she was hearing from her daughter, whom she loved dearly. Kay grabbed a cup of water, paused a second, and threw it into May's face. May did not understand what happened that day; hearing little sweet Kay yell at her was shocking. May knew it was not normal; in a short time, she was changing into someone else. May decided to get her help, so she took her to counseling for the next three years.

Every Thanksgiving, they had to go to Toby and Sue's house. When Sue was alive, the family visited every year to share hope and love and respect. When Kay was in first and second grade, May had to talk with Kay to make sure that Otto and Kay understood how to behave. May remembered what Toby did when Otto was three years old; she explained that they should not argue with their grandparents. They should always say thank you and smile; that was the way to show respect. May believe in educating them earlier rather than late, and that was how she grew up in her country. May did not want to be hurt by Toby again. After many years, May saw how Toby hurt everyone in the family; when he would exchange views, he would argue regardless of who he spoke to, babbling foolish talk about n—s and Jews, but May made sure he did not hurt Otto or Kay.

When Kay was six years old, they were getting ready to go visit Toby and Sue on Thanksgiving. May laid out clothes for Kay to wear, but she did not want to go. She refused to wear the clothes May picked out. May lost her temper, grabbed a coat hanger, and whipped Kay on her hip. It was a hurtfulness that May still remembers to this day. May apologized and told Kay how sorry and ashamed she was. May cried a long time and said to her, "Please, I love you, and please forgive me. I am so sorry."

That day, May focused on loving her more and giving her more attention. Kay should have been getting attention from Joe, but May had to be a father and mother at the same time. It was not easy; it was a burden. May thought she must not stop loving her as much as she could.

Later, after counseling, Kay found her thoughts were fighting, raising unpleasant sensations produced by Toby.

She explained to May, "Mom, every time we go to Grandfather and Grandmother's house, I do not want to sit on Grandfather's lap."

May wondered what she was trying to tell her and asked, "Why don't you want to sit on Grandfather's lap?"

Kay gave an answer that no mother wants to hear, and every mother should pay attention when a child says what this child said. Kay explained what happened every time she sat on Toby's lap: "Every time I sit on his lap, his legs are shaking, and he squeezes and hugs me too tight. Something hard touches me under my bottom, and I do not like it." She took a breath for a minute and added, "And I do not like how he talks to Dad!"

May heard Kay ask for help and believed that she was suffering and in pain. How much more could May take? Toby's actions were a liability; he had exposed others to harm long before May met him. May could only do one thing: she must keep her daughter from being hurt any more than she had been and get her counseling for what had happened. Now May understood Kay's anger and need for attention. Kay was hurt and stressed.

May said, "If you do not want to go see Grandfather, then you do not have to." May held Kay's hand, hugged her, and quietly said, "I am so sorry. I should not have spanked you. I love you with all my heart. I will make sure Grandfather never puts you on his lap again." May cried many nights to herself; she did not let Joe know, and every day she told Kay, "I love you, and you are very special."

May knew she needed to protect her; it was something that had to be done. May thought she would share with Kay the old mirror she brought from her country. It was not the best, but May had that mirror since she was a child; her mother had given it to her. She had lots of good memories of being with her friends.

Kay loved to play in front of the mirror with her friends. That mirror gave her hope that her future would be bright. At the same time, she might not forget what happened, but she did grow out of being stressed by Toby. She no longer had to go see a counselor when she became a young girl. She was a happy young girl, playing with her friends in front of the mirror, dressing up like a movie star, making funny faces, looking at each other laughing and giggling like happy, normal young girls. When Kay looked at her reflection in the mirror, it reminded her of her mother as a young girl; May looked at Kay as a beautiful young woman. The old mirror gave life-long lessons; mother had hopes for daughter, and they loved each other.

When Kay grew up, she became engaged to her high school sweetheart. Kay was ready to move in with her future husband. When she was ready to move, Kay was attached to the old mirror and politely asked May, "Mom, can I take that old mirror with me?"

"Yes, dear sweetheart, you can take that old mirror."

Kay was glad and happy to take that old mirror with her. May thought that since she had just built a new home, that old mirror may not look good in her house, but it was a personal choice. She said to Kay, "Dear, that old mirror is getting old; the mother of pearl is getting loose, it has scratches all over, and the colors are faded and dull. Wouldn't you like to have a new mirror in your new home?"

She answered solemnly, "No, Mom, I would rather have that old mirror, if it is okay with you."

"You can take it with you."

Kay said, "Mom, I might be moving out of your home, but when I look at that old mirror in my closet, I will see you every day, and I love you, Mom."

When May heard that, tears were wetting her cheeks and she was humbled. Moreover, for her, that old mirror had been given to her by her precious and valuable mother, and she shared feelings and affection with her daughter. May treasured every day and their close relationship. To this day, Kay is still married to Tony, her high school sweetheart; they are doing good, and most of all, her future is bright.

To a loving daughter:

> To have a daughter, brightens the day with happiness.
>
> To have a daughter, brings hope to the future.
>
> To have a daughter, grows hope and love.
>
> To have a daughter, brings tears of joy and laughter.
>
> Without a daughter, the spirit no longer lives.
>
> To have a daughter, makes life eager.
>
> To have a daughter, teaches truth and respect.
>
> To have a daughter is a blessing.

CHAPTER 19
Toby Teaches His Son and Grandchildren

All children need a father's love and care. How many fathers and mothers give their children enough attention? May knew; she grew up under her stepfather's care. She became a self-contained person who always told the truth. If a child does not have a father, they could lose hope in a positive future. May believed that every child should have a father and mother.

But Joe was a father who acted like a child, which made it harder for May. Joe was like a grown child who did not know how to be a real parent. He did not have responsibility, he did not know how to pay the bills or how to earn income, he did not know where the money was coming from, and so on. Joe was not accountable; he chose to be that way, but when you have a child, then a man's life should change, a child should grow into an adult. Adults are morally accountable for their actions and are capable of rational conduct; they are responsible. A man who cannot stand on his two feet makes it harder for his children to discover their own identity.

Going back to Toby, he is not a good father. Toby was known as a big guy with a bad temper. The family learned from grandfather and father, and then the children became who they became. As time went by, Joe learned from Toby; he became irrational, imprecise, narrow-minded, and prejudiced. And he could not be proud of it. Toby should have taught Joe and Dan, but teaching children how to learn and grow is a big issue that no mother should ignore.

For many years, Junk lived with his grandfather, Toby. He worked here and there, earning some income, while living in his grandfather's home. When Junk came home, he would hear his grandfather insult people, calling them n—s and Jews, and saying someone could not get a job as a trucker. He heard this every day and it became programmed into his mind, and the grandson wanted to follow in his grandfather's footsteps. Junk began to act and talk like Toby. He was hateful and was reluctant to be around Muslims, and he was uncaring, indolent, and slothful and made comments about how they are in the way in his work place. May could not, would not, must not be accepted.

Visiting Toby's house always caused an argument between Joe and May. Every visit, they would bring dinner to Toby and Sue; their favorite food was pizza and Kentucky-fried chicken. When they finished dinner, Toby would ask Sue, "Where is my apple pie?" His voice was demanding, showing off in front of Joe to demonstrate that he is the man.

Sue answered softly and coyly, "Apple pie has been cooking, and it is ready to eat."

She cut the apple pie and gave Toby a slice; he took a bite of pie and complained about the crust, saying, "Why does this pie crust have a burned spot?"

The way he said this to her was not nice. May could not take the way he acted to Sue, how his voice was threatening and ominously irritated. May did not want to hear his adversity to Sue and said to him, "There is nothing the matter with this apple pie, the top portion of the oven is hot and the bottom is not as hot, but the apple pie is edible!"

This is true about any baking oven. He did not like to hear this but he ate the apple pie and sat quietly back in the recliner. May knew he was going to make a comment about the apple pie. He began to degrade the car makers from Japan. On and on, he did not tire and would not stop. He sat there doing so all day. May tried to ignore Toby's insults. Toby did not like that May was ignoring his comments. Joe and May did not want to make a scene; they had to live in their house.

Joe saw how his father treated his mother and degraded other women. Joe began to carry on like Toby, and as a husband and father to two children, Joe could not show mercy to his children or his wife. It was hurtful and could not be forgiven. Sometimes, Joe resembled his father. May could not believe that Joe acted that way with her and Otto and Kay.

On weekends, the children would visit with May. Every time they visited, May tried to cook and communicate with them, because children need attention. May had no education in how to cook, but she learned in high school by cooking at home five days a week. She learned how to cook rice and fry rice and more. After the children married and left home, they would come home with hope and love; Mom cooked their favorite dinner and they would talk about how life was good.

Before that, Joe did not know the expression "bring children into the world"; it was not his job to lead the children where they were going, but he automatically transmitted Toby's personality with a bad mood. Whenever he put his lunch carrier on top of the counter, they knew he had a bad day and would not bother him.

He wanted to hear from the children first, and then the children saw that he had a bad day. They said to Joe, "Hi, Dad, how are you?" Otto and Kay were trying to be as nice as they could be and not bother him. Joe answered with a cold voice, "Hi, how are you doing?"

His voice sounded annoyed and distressed. May tried to follow his annoying habit and lead the family. It was almost working, and she smiled and joked as she cooked, showing how she learned to cook fried rice. BOOL-GO-GEE was his favorite dinner, so she also made that. The children devoured it down with the veggies and rice; the BOOL-GO-GEE comforted May, the tension from Joe began to decrease.

Joe could not learn to control his temper. It goes on to this present day. He cannot tell his children, "I love you." If a father cannot show affection and love to his children, then how can they learn affection and love? How are they going to show their own children love and affection? Joe and May would often visit Toby. May often asked him many things. "Can you tell us about your grandfather?" she asked. But Toby did not answer completely, most of the time he shied away from the subject and did not want to answer.

One day May asked Toby, "How was your relationship with your dad?"

He carefully answered, "I never had an intimate relationship with my dad, but when we worked, we worked together okay; when we worked, we did not have a problem."

This explains how he became bitter and had no direction from his father and did not learn how to be affectionate to his wife and children and grandchildren. Junk had no role model for his life. Junk grew up under his grandfather, and Toby was a hero to Junk. Toby showed no affection and love to Sue; he saw that. He could not see himself as a drug dearer, an alcoholic, or someone driving without a license.

Otto tried hard to accept who he was; he loved his grandfather and father, but it was hard to accept who they were. May taught him that education has to be first, but at the same time, he looked at Toby and Joe, who were from two different worlds, but Joe and Toby ignored him and did not care. May fought and fought to give Otto's life direction; she pleaded with Joe, "Your son needs help from his father, not his mother. I cannot be father and mother at the same time, please help your son!"

May begged and pleaded, but Joe had no response; it went in one ear and out the other, and the next day, nothing happened. He had no feeling, no way to show love; this is what he learned from Toby. May fought back with her opinion of the importance of being a mother to Otto, trying to do what she could to help. She argued with Joe and criticized him, saying, "A father's job is to take his son to the park, play ball with him, help with his homework, and most of all, a father shows affection and love to his family; you are not doing any of those things. What is the matter with you, @#@#%?"

May came down and pointed her finger at Toby and Joe, saying, "I hear you, you do not have to speak, your @#@#% father Toby showed you how to abuse women, your mother, and you have been abused by him, therefore, you do not know how? Too bad, mister, grow out of it and become a man when you bring a child into the world; do you understand that, @#@#?"

Her temper and anger came from too much pressure and responsibility for Otto. In her country, she would not yell at her spouse, and calling names would not be accepted. One must respect and uphold the household.

Joe looked at May, shocked; he did not want to hear more than what she said and tried to stop her from saying more. He said, "I hear you; stop the nonsense. You are using foul language; you do not have to call me names."

After calling Joe names, May calmed down and thought, *What is next for Otto?* Hard times will fade away, and joy will take over when the time comes; she must never give up until the finish line.

From father Toby to son Joe to grandson Otto, they inherited more than their color—it was who they were. All the same, Otto admitted that he saw his grandfather play life on his own. He was not a good man to his family; he abused, teased, and provoked them, and used his children to get what he wanted. Whoever he was around, he would lie and cheat and pass hatred and bitterness to his children and grandchildren. If Otto chose to follow in his grandfather's footsteps, then May could not stop it, but May could stand with her feet firmly on the ground. Her devotion to Otto was worth the effort at this time; when time went by, Otto would learn and move on to the future.

Toby had a short memory and did not know when his grandfather died or where he came from. But all children are born with colors of the rainbow. Many children born in America are biracial. Parents must be careful they do not lose their culture, identification, and individuality. On the other hand, the children think civilized thoughts and blend in with their family's gathering. Biracial children could not take either side; they meet in the middle and sometimes it works out as well as it can. Having children and marriage should be open-minded. Biracial children are smart and beautiful. They have open minds and can get along in general, but they can be hurt, confused, and mystified.

Sometimes, their mother tells them one thing, and then their father tells them the opposite, so they will be confused and puzzled. Some do not accept their identity. Many children have problems and rebel against their parents, like Otto did. May knew that Toby made it harder to work with Otto, rather than easier. The grandchildren wanted to be with their grandfather, like most children do. Grandfathers have wisdom to tell stories; children should love and be comforted to see their grandfather. For this grandfather, that is not the case.

Otto visited with Toby when he could, but Toby had a problem with Otto. Otto rode a motorcycle when the weather was sunny. When Toby saw this, he complained, "It looks like a motorcycle gang."

He joked about the motorcycle. Otto's job could be demanding, but Toby did not care how he got there; he commented to Otto, "He wins his job, nowadays he has to work harder than we ever did."

Otto could not take Toby as a role model. He saw Toby as someone to stay away from. He had no interest in visiting his grandfather. Instead, not knowing him gave him peace of mind. Kay had stayed away from Toby for a long time. She wanted to be given attention as a glamorous, charismatic girl. Kay knew her mom loved her, but May did not know how to read her mind. At the same time, her relationship with Toby was no longer inappropriate. But Kay was smart and proud. Any mother would be proud and share what was going on in her mind about what Toby did to Kay; it could have been utter pandemonium. May had no words for Toby, instead Kay stayed away from him.

Remember when Otto was hurt by his wife? He learned from Toby as well as from Joe to demand attention from a woman for pleasure and sex, and he believed that men were superior over women. Otto began to rebel like a child. He heard Toby blame others, and Joe complained every time Otto saw him, starting with the job he had and where he was. Otto did not know where he wanted to go and what to do with his life; he was lost.

May asked Otto, "What are you good at?"

Otto answered, "I am good with math and numbers!"

May had a good idea and told Otto, "Numbers can be done in many jobs, it can be a doctor's job, or accountant and so on, therefore, you must choose what you are good at. At the same time, accounting can be used in life to know where your money is going!"

Otto heard and chose to be an accountant. After two years, he earned a degree and had a good job in with a corporation. That was before Otto married Miss Hock. Otto went out of town one or two days a week for his job. His wife was hardnosed and objected to his work.

His wife said, "Why do you have to be an accountant? You should be in business, you have to go back and get a degree in business."

So to please her, he went back to college two more years to get another degree, but he never got a job in business. In three years of marriage, he blamed May for becoming an accountant. To this day, Otto has blamed her that he has an accounting job; he thinks he should be a business leader in some other company. At this present time, he is working at a big corporation. He started as an accountant and now he is an analyst. The company promoted him. May was proud that Otto reached higher ground. Without the job as an accountant and his experience and knowledge, how would he get a job as an analyst?

One day visiting with May and Kay, Otto said proudly, "I am no longer an accountant, I am an analyst!" He wanted May to hear, and at the same time let her know he no longer had to hear her say, "My son is an accountant!"

Otto was unfeeling and stone cold. Where did the abuse come from? He saw the way Toby treated Sue and saw how unyielding Joe was; Otto did not learn how to accommodate. May had to work harder to accept her way of thinking. May would be proud of her son, whether he became a trucker or analyst, no matter who he is. The only thing May could do was stand by what he wanted to be. Furthermore, he must respect women in the future. May pushed Otto to have an education.

May was not in denial; she said to Otto, "I am going to make sure you go to college; you will have more education than I have, and you will have a better life than I have; the more you are educated, the greater you will survive!"

He must not take a short cut; short cuts are failure, and failure is no option to May. May had good times and bad times with Otto, but she let go of him and when he needs help he will call her. He is a grown young man, and she will let him decide his future; she will stay out of her son's life.

One time, he was catching a cold and called May. "Mom," he said, "I think I am catching a cold, I do not know how to get over this cold." He called for help and let May know he did not forget her, that he loved her.

That time he did not think about his grandfather's short temper; May showed Otto how she cared for him and loved him. May showed Otto a mother's love to her child is powerful, it restores hope and the trust a child needs to feel.

When they are raised with malice and pathology, pity and sadness, children become voraciously materialistic. Evil sees evil do, grandfather Toby showed the family how not to treat a child or grandchild. Christmas was a holiday for all children, with joy and hope they pray, thinking that dreams will come true. Mothers and fathers tell their children to be good, they behave, and parents want to give them more gifts with love. But if a child sees what comes on Christmas Day, if the dream was not what they hoped it to be, the child will experience betrayal.

A child learns how play with Mom and Dad, who say, "You be good; if you cry, Santa Claus is not going to come."

The child tries not to cry and becomes an angel. They are given toys and clothes from Mom and Dad working hard to earn money. Up to age five, they believe Santa was coming to see them. As the child grows, they begin to not believe in Santa; Christmas becomes a play time. The growing child playing on Christmas can be more than betrayed, more abuse, showing who they are as the real person emerges.

For years, Otto and Kay heard from May, "Christmas is coming, you guys be good."

Every year at Christmas, May would give them gifts. Then Otto and Kay got married and moved out on their own, which was good. Again, every year Otto and Kay came to May's house for Christmas. If it was not Christmas, she might not see Otto and Kay. Unless they were having a problem, then they would call May asking for help, and May would try her best to help as best as she knew.

One year, before Otto's birthday, he started to come to May's house once a week, acting like he loved his mom and asking for forgiveness, saying, "Mom, I am sorry if I was a bad boy, can you forgive me?" Overall, Otto knew how to play on May's emotions with malevolence.

Christmas was coming, and after that, Kay's birthday and her husband's birthday were coming up. May was visiting and shopping and ready to please her children.

May loved her son, and she was glad he was coming around; she told Otto, "I am so happy to see you, and I love you. I have no anger; every child makes mistakes, and I have too. I was not a perfect child when I was young; there is no reason to apologize."

May hugged him, pleased and delighted to see him. Everything was going to be good, and she wondered where and when they should have his birthday dinner. She asked, "What would you like to have for your birthday dinner?"

Otto was glad May asked what he wanted to have for dinner, and he answered clearly, "You know what I want, because I would like to have Korean B-G-G and lots of veggies."

May knew what he wanted but she asked anyway; she said, "Okay, that is what you want, then it is done."

May was glad it was working out with her son. She missed all those months, but now Otto was happy and said good-bye to May at the door. May choked on her throat, and her tears were wetting her cheeks; she hoped to see him again. Cooking birthday dinners for her children was the most pleasing time for May. When dinner was over, they talked about exchanging Christmas gifts. All agreed to meet at May's house at a certain time. Otto brought his girlfriend to May's house. When Otto did not have a girlfriend, he came home alone. May thought she should go out for lunch with Otto to cheer him up, which she did. May thought she could have a good time with her son, and she paid more than she could afford, yet Otto mocked his mother about the food they had and made bad complaints. May ignored him and tried to have a good time; that was one of the few times they went out to eat.

That day, May felt uncomfortable to sit with her son, yet she was thinking, *It is going to be okay; he is my son, and he is not going to hurt his mother.*

After dinner, as they drove home, May thought positively. Later, she was waiting for Kay, getting all the gifts ready to exchange while Otto and Joe took a nap. May was in the kitchen, she could not help thinking, "Today is a children's holiday, try to grow as a good mother."

Kay had a good time, so did her husband, and Otto looked like he was having a good time, but May saw a dark shadow passing over his face; something was not right. May was extremely careful; she did not agitate him and waited for it to be over. Otto and Kay had a good time; May was glad the holiday was over and set up the time for Kay's birthday dinner.

The following week, everyone had to go to work. There was too much snow on the ground, causing problems with going home, and May did not want the children to visit her house that day.

Two week later, it was Kay's birthday and she went to see both her and Tony, her husband. Soon Otto called; Joe answered and said, "I thought you went home."

Otto said, "I had to work a little late and do not think I am going to make it to Kay's today."

Joe said to Otto, "Okay, please be careful going home, and here is your mom."

Joe gave the phone to May. Joe could not talk to Otto for more than one minute. Whenever Otto called, Joe could not communicate with him and would give the phone to May as soon as he could.

May asked Otto, "Hi, son, how are you doing? I thought you might have gone home; are you working late?"

Otto answered in a happy tone, "Yes, I was a little late coming into work, and I am making up lost time."

At that moment, she did not hear Otto's statement. May was thinking about having dinner at Kay and her husband's house. Kay's husband was out of town for the first time and had been gone from Monday to Friday. It was the first time they had been apart from each other in eleven years of marriage plus three years of dating.

At the same time, Otto was telling May his friend was getting married out of state; he asked May if she wanted to go to the wedding. May did not know that person; it was a friend who was renting out Otto's room, and he was a foreigner. Otto asked if she wanted to drive all the way out of state.

May did not want to drive that far and come home two days later;

it was too much driving and sitting in the car. Otto was upset that she could not go with him.

The following week, it was Kay's birthday dinner, and Otto asked, "Can my friend come?"

Kay answered that it was okay, but May thought, *This is the day we are having dinner for Kay's birthday with her husband.*

May thought, as a mother, she needed to help her daughter deal with the stress of being away from her husband after many years of marriage; she thought Kay had a lot of worry and stress. That snowy day, May told Otto, "It is not a good idea for your friend to be there."

That was that; Otto was looking for an argument and wanted to show his emotions and his ego, and he yelled at May like Joe and Toby, "You and Kay are thinking a negative attitude that it is going to be a failure, then it is not going to be fulfilled. When I went to college, if you had a negative attitude, it would be fulfilled! Do not worry, he is not coming this week!"

May said to her son, "I have not talked to your sister Kay; what does this have to do with failure and fulfill?"

"I say do not worry about it; he is not coming!"

Again, May tried to explain to Otto, "Kay is my daughter, and I have the right to help my daughter. She is under a lot of stress, and looking at both sides, her husband Tony has to leave after dinner, and I do not think it is a good idea to finish dinner and rush out and leave Kay's house—and it is not a good feeling. I want you to look at both sides."

Otto would not stop arguing. May thought it was not a good idea to argue on the phone and cut him off, saying to Otto, "I am not going to argue on the phone; I will see you tomorrow at ten o'clock."

The next morning, May was all ready to go to Kay's house dinner with gifts. She thought, *Today hope begins and looking for the future.* The phone rang at eight thirty; it was Otto, standing at the back door and calling, "I am at your back door!"

May saw Otto at the back door with his phone; she opened the door and said to herself, *I thought you would be here at ten o'clock.*

May let Otto in with a smile; at the same time she was talking to her son and putting down the phone. As Otto came into the kitchen, he started to say to May, "I saw someone selling food in the street …"

May did not hear the end of his sentence; she only heard him mention the food vendor, and she thought she would try to communicate with Otto, that he had forgotten what had happened last night; today was the new beginning, and she said to Otto, "I do not care about the food vendor. I have a bigger dream than that."

May meant that she was saving every penny for the future with his sister's dream. May had no problem with a food vendor.

May tried to explain that some had success as a food vendor on the West Coast but this was the East Coast. May did explain that Otto's job had a good future wherever he wanted to go.

Otto asked May, "What time does the mall open?" At the same time, he was looking for something to eat; he always came to her house hungry, looking in the refrigerator and in the cabinets for any kind of food.

May, trying to please Otto, said, "Here, I made it last night; have some soup with rice."

Otto heated up the soup, added some hot sauce, and started to eat. May could not read Otto's mind at that time. She tried to answer Otto and tell him what time the shopping mall opened, but it started an argument; she asked, "Why do you have to go to the shopping mall? They open on Sundays at eleven o'clock or noon."

He answered with a scratchy sounding voice, "I did not get any gifts for him and I need to go to Lowes and get matching pots."

When May heard the scratchy sound of his voice, she got a feeling in her backbone of chilling fear. Sometimes, when he was eating, he would think about how he was going to argue with May. It was a perfect time to show May who he was, and he knew his friend was not coming.

May was facing the front window and washing her hands, and he was eating soup. Yet May turned around and looked at Otto's face; she saw his face was in the bowl eating and at the same time talking to May. May saw Otto's face changing, when she saw that, she thought, "What is the matter? Is something wrong?"

Otto heard May's thought and became a malefactor, and he yelled at May, "So your dream is bigger than mine! You do not care what I want to do, and your dream is better than mine!"

May heard Otto screaming; she did not know what to think, what to say. "What are you talking about?" she asked. "I do not understand your anger."

Otto said, "I would like to be a food vendor, and then you say your dream is bigger than mine!"

May understood then, but the first time he did not say clearly he was going to be a food vendor. She said carefully, "You did not say clearly you were going to be a food vendor, and I did not hear you; when you talked you slurred the words, you did not finish the last word, and I was confused about what you wanted to do with that food, because I had a dream and it has nothing to do with your food."

Otto looked at May and screamed, "You do not care about anything but yourself; your dream is bigger than mine! F— you! F— you. Do you understand that?"

Mom heard f— and f—, and she was sad and said to Otto, "You say what? F— you?"

Smiling, Otto said, "Yes, f— you! And drive yourself to Tony and Kim's house!"

Otto slammed the door as hard as he could and went out, driving away so fast the tires were spinning. May stood there thinking, *I did not ask him to drive me there, and why did he say "F— me"?*

She had difficulty understanding what happened in such a short time; it was a stupid act. She said, "This is not the first time. It has been going on for many years; I must calm down and get Kay's dinner ready."

Kay stopped by and asked, "What happened with Otto?"

May was ready to go to Kay's house and have her birthday dinner. May could not explain to Kay; instead, she burst into tears thinking back on Otto's harsh words.

Christmas and birthdays are a time to let go of who you love most. January begins with hope and love, and what happened yesterday was a bad dream; all that matters is right now.

May said to Kay, "No reason for me to get mad. I am ready to have some food. I have been cooking, so let us go to your place and cook this food, I know your husband had to leave this afternoon."

May hoped Otto would be at Kay's house, but it did not happen.

Kay was sad, but she was a mature young woman. May loved to

see her and the hope was bright; she gave her a hug and said to Kay, "I love you, and the hope begins now."

It is not about birthdays or him or her, as a mother pays attention to what a child needs; sometimes that is not good enough in the child's mind, yet mothers and fathers give their children enough attention as parents. No matter what they take or give, there is always some agreement we must have between child and parent.

To the son I love and the daughter I adore

First snow fall purity:

Let it flow, let it flow, and let it flow.

First snow brings purity to soul and mind.

Let the old dust brush upon your shoulder.

Let first snow fall purity sit on your shoulder.

Decentralize your lungs with first snow fall purity.

Take a deep breath. Decentralize with first snow fall purity.

Let the heart muscle pump.

Decentralize with first snow fall purity.

Let the soul and mind begin to heal.

Let it flow, let it flow, and let it flow.

Purity of first snow fall.

Let it flow, let it flow, and let it flow.

CHAPTER 20
Getting to Know Joe's Family

Getting to know Joe's family was a pain. From grandparent to parent, they were immature family members who discriminated against the children you loved and said unfavorable things, provoking bigotry and prejudice.

Going back overseas, marriage was based on respect. Most marriages were arranged by both sides, mother and father. The expectation was that it would be accepted and husband and wife would learn to love each other. With having children, a father must take care of his family's needs. In an arranged marriage, the wife stayed home, most of the time. In a sense, the husband worked and took care of business. People often lived with their grandparents, sometime two families under one roof. The husband was responsible for the main household, and the children learned from their father how to prepare for the future. And the grandparents helped the children to behave, sharing their wisdom as grandparents. Most children obey their grandparent as well as parents.

The most important belief in Asia is the belief in the family tree and the extended family. Extended families lived together in a big house. They often visited their mom and dad. Brothers or sisters easily helped each other and their parents. Most grandchildren loved their grandparents; if one grandparent went away, the children learned from their other grandparents and their parents to carry on and take care of the extended family. Family members respect each other and teach the extended family that life goes on.

In Korea, holidays are festive celebrations. May remembered her childhood. It was the most dazzling time for a child to have fun and learn how to carry on; her aunt taught her to respect and worship religious supplications that looked to the new year and were thankful for what they had right now and in the future. Every year, May's mother, Kim, took her to a tailor shop and had a dress made to wear; it took two weeks to make. Kim would take out all the silverware and polish it. She bought many veggies, meat (beef, pork, and chicken), and seafood as well as fruit. They also had grains, rice, beans, and more. She cooked so much that they did not have to cook for two or three weeks. The night before Thanksgiving, the family went to a bath house and cleaned all the dust on their shoulders to get ready for Thanksgiving morning. In the morning, her grandfather and grandmother sat and waited for the religious ritual to begin.

Kim had cooked and cleaned the house with care (two or three of May's cousins also helped); she then served her aunt and grandfather and grandmother. Grandfather and grandmother would kneel down and touch their foreheads down on the floor three times, about five to ten seconds, and then they offered thanks to their mom and dad and aunts who had passed away, thanking them for making it through the year alive and well, and then asking for help in the coming year for their children and grandchildren. It only took about twenty minutes to finish.

Grandfather and Grandmother offered wine to each other and then began to eat. Older people are respected so much that they are the first to sip the wine, and the children come next. After the religious worship was finished, the children would devour the food. They had waited a long time, watching their grandparents worship; the children were hungry from the aroma of food that they did not eat every day: beef sticks and many other foods; the aroma was delicious, but the children waited patiently. After all that, the children were hungry but they were as happy as can be. After devouring all that food, holiday festivities began. Fathers were drinking wine with friends and playing games in the corner of the house, as happy as a child in a school yard. You could hear farmers dancing and singing; the nation was happy with positive thoughts for the next year and the next generation.

Toby spent Thanksgiving at his house every year until Sue's health began to decline. After all, this was his house and his family, he imagined. However, he did what he wanted to do with his family, leading to richer or poorer. There was not any worship or anything valuable to teach the grandchildren or children or others. Sue cooked turkey, mashed potatoes, green beans, gravy, and homemade noodles. After the turkey was cooked, they all sat at the dining table and ate. They did not care, most of all the subject of Thanksgiving was not important. Instead, they talked about Christmas and what presents they should get and give. Toby had to be the center of attention, and Lake agreed and sat eating the turkey and homemade noodles Sue cooked all morning. After dinner was eaten, the grandchildren devoured the turkey, and then the apple pie or pumpkin pie for dessert. The pies were loaded with sugar. Eating all that sugar, the family began to tire from overeating, grandparent and aunts were taking a nap.

The children played some games, and then they sat around the table for hours and ate pies and cakes with sugary coke or sugary iced tea to wash them down. They did not know that Toby always played with Kay. She often had to sit on his lap.

Toby would pick Kay up and say, "Sit on my lap. How is my granddaughter doing? Let me give you a hug." He would squeeze her and kiss her on the cheek.

Kay did not like to sit on his lap or be squeezed or kissed. She tried to get off Toby's lap, but he would say, "Sit still, little girl!"

Kay was scared and unhappy whenever that happened. But she sat quietly and unobtrusively; she listened to her grandfather and looked for a chance to get away from his leg. Toby showed Kay how to sit on his leg, and then he began to move his leg up and down, shaking and squeezing while he talked to her.

At the same time, Kay did not know what her grandfather was doing; she only knew it was not comfortable sitting on his lap. She had no voice to say, "No, Grandfather, you are squeezing too hard; let go of me."

Kay was frightened and just sat there, trying to get off his lap. Kay did a good job not crying or screaming at her ill-tempered grandfather. At that time, she was only three years old and did not know why he was squeezing her every time she sat on his lap.

With that, May did not know what he was doing to her until almost five years later, after she talked to the counselor and Kay told her she did not want to go see her grandfather. May was hurt and did not know how to solve the problem; she took the burden on her shoulders, and now is the time to tell what she learned about the perplexing family.

After Kay told May she did not want to go to see her grandfather, May said to Kay, "I am so sorry; what happened is completely wrong. I did not see what was going on. I thought he was giving you love like a grandfather, but I was wrong, and if you do not want to go there, then you do not have to go there, and I love you. Please forgive me."

It was the old Thanksgiving time to visit with family, no children's hope to look for, just Toby's perverted visit with daughter and granddaughter and great-granddaughter, playing to the sexual desire of a pervert. Every Christmas going to his house was a nuisance and a bother. The little gifts they would receive were not worth attending. Overall, it was a family gathering. At the same time, going to see the family should have been a happy time, and they should have been eager to see their grandparents.

Again, Sue cooked ham and some veggies with sweet cookies and fruit cake. They also made cakes and cookies with lots of sugar and white flour. Otto's curiosity was normal for his age, but it got him in trouble, and Toby slapped him. May never forgot this to today, even though it was a long time ago and she should let go of it. But the mental anguish makes it feel like yesterday.

Every time they went to visit their grandparents, Otto and Kay always sat with May. Otto and Kay always stayed together, and May did not let Toby hurt Otto or Kay. She watched wherever the children were. They did not stay longer than they had to. Otto watched wherever his young sister Kay sat.

Others always saw this, and Dan and Lake pointed to May and Joe and said, "You guys always sit together?" They thought it was strange to see. Lake did not accept May. When May met Lake, Otto had just been born and Joe was still overseas. May was alone and living with Toby and Sue.

That year, Lake's husband left her with her two children. She did not know where he went. Toby and Sue tried to help her and brought Christmas gifts to the grandchildren. May did not know how to help her. May herself was alone and did not know how to wrap a gift box. Toby and Sue brought some toys and were trying to wrap them with Christmas paper. Lake thought that May was going to help, but she just sat and watched how they did it. They did not know that May did not know how to wrap presents; Toby said, "She could help, but she is not going to."

When May heard this, she thought, *What are you saying? Did you bring me here to work? You are thinking I do not understand English. Why are you talking like I cannot hear?*

May was quiet and looked to see how her son was doing. The grandchildren were in school and had a time to organize gifts for the other children.

Then Sue asked May, "Would you like your hair cut? Lake can cut your hair."

At that time, May had long, flowing hair; she wondered whether she should let Lake cut her hair. After she had her hair cut, they all laughed and laughed.

May wondered why they were laughing; she thought, *What did I do wrong?*

That day, she found out that the haircut would not stay and they were laughing at her haircut; they thought that it was a fun thing to do.

May looked suspicious at that moment and thought, *They are creepy people; somehow they are creepy. They are creeps.*

Otto grew faster than May could believe. One day, she asked Lake if she would like to babysit him, thinking it would be good for him to get to know his aunt. That was the first day May let Otto spend time with Lake. Five hours later, she brought Otto back home with a bandage on his finger; his fingernail was almost lost. There was broken glass in the sandbox, and the broken glass cut his fingernail almost to the bone. May was angry and did not trust her. *She will not babysit my child again,* May said to herself.

As time passed, May did not think of all these untrustworthy things going on. After Joe had worked for the same company for one year, they were invited to a family dinner. There was a swimming pool and everyone had a good time. Joe was not into swimming and neither was May.

At the same time, some friends were visiting, and Lake was drunk and in and out of the swimming pool. All of a sudden, she jumped into Joe's lap and started to put her hands on his chest, rubbing and touching him. She said, "Last time I saw you, you did not have hair, and now you have grown, and you have lots of hair on your chest. Let me touch your hair."

She stuck her hands on his chest and rubbed and wiggled side to side as she sat in the same position that she would sit on Toby's lap many years earlier; she thought she would play with her little brother's lap and do something exciting.

Lake looked at May for a reaction. Joe was uncomfortable with this unwanted sexual attention; it was more than oppressive.

He grabbed her hand, put it back onto her lap, and said, "You must stop. This is not nice; you are drunk and crazy." Joe was angry and embarrassed at the same time; his face was red as a beet.

After a few seconds, she stopped and went into the house; May looked at Lake and said, "You are a corrupt person; what is the matter with you?" Lake looked like she was enjoying the attention.

Joe was bothered because Lake showed such disrespect in front of May. She had no boundaries; she was a home-wrecker, and she did not mind. She sexually pleased her father by sitting on his lap for many years. May did not ask Joe why Lake behaved that way. May thought she was in a trusted marriage; jealousy should not be an issue with her husband. Therefore, she must let go of it. Do not compete with someone so brainless.

When May was pregnant with Kay, Lake was able to buy a new home through a government housing program,. She had an open house to introduce everyone to her new home. The house was nice and had fresh paint and three bathrooms.

May and Joe thought to give her attention about how nice her home was; they said to her, "This house is nice; how did you get it?"

Her answer was sharply bitter; it was the chance she wanted to tell May what was on her mind: "You can have a house like this if you divorce your husband!"

May thought it was a bad idea, and she was hurt. That was what Lake wanted to see. May was young and did not know what this family was like, and she tried to work as a family and not be bitter. Joe knew that Lake and May had a complex relationship as sister and sister-in-law. May was also fighting to keep her children safe as well. May needed and should have had some kind of help from the family, but she did not ask to take over Lake's place as a daughter to Toby or Sue.

Lake should not have thought that May was going to take over her place. May asked Joe, "I do not understand what she is afraid of. I am not going to take her parents. I just do not know how I can tell her I do love her and want to work together if we can."

At that moment, Joe needed to tell her what his sister told him before he left to go overseas; she told Joe, "If you marry an Asian woman, I will never speak to you, understand that?"

When May heard that, she asked Joe, "Why doesn't she like Asian women? What have I done that she does not like me?" Joe had no answer but said briefly, "Maybe it has to do with the photo Toby carries from overseas of an Asian woman; my father has nightmares from what happened; he has night sweats and horrifying dreams."

May heard and paused a second; then she said, "I understand your father's dream; what he did was wrong, killing an innocent person, and he needs to come out and admit that he was wrong to kill that person, it was a mistake, and he is sorry. Then the dream might go away. That still does not answer why she does not like me."

Her husband sat quietly and said, "I cannot say what my sister's problem is. I have talked to her and asked her to please stop her animosity toward you, that you have done nothing to hurt her and have nothing to do with Dad's problem. I've asked her to please give you some respect, but she is not going to—she's going to be nasty again and again because you're smart and beautiful, that is why."

It did not matter to Lake; in her mind, May was going to be replace the Asian woman in the photo her father carried. Lake and May had a complex relationship. Every time Lake had a problem, she ran to Toby, and she never forgot he promised Lake that he would take care of her. Lake kept coming back and coming back to Toby when she had a problem, and she lived in his house rent free—she did not even have to cook.

It is perplexing, as years go by, most people do learn and move on with their lives. Dan was living in another state and soon wanted to move back home to live near Toby and Sue and Lake as well as Joe. His excuse was he wanted to be close to family and have more time with them. It is acceptable and a good thing for a family to be close and unified. He had been away for almost twenty-five years. Since then, many things changed. He did not see what was going on with the family; rather, he heard about "he did this" and "she did that." He did not know what was true or not; he just heard rumors. Most of the time, what we hear are rumors.

May said, "If you want to believe what you hear from someone, it may not be true, unless you see it with your own eyes." May knew they had no idea what she had seen and thought.

One day, Dan and June invited May and Joe to spend time at their house. Dan and June could be a little proud of their success by bragging about where they lived and what jobs he had. Dan had retired from an airline after working as a pilot and flying big airplanes. He had a lot of success, and June never had to work in her life. She was a homemaker; she could cook sweets, cookies, cakes, and more. But at the same time, was she smart? You be the judge.

While they visited, the two brothers were talking about how their jobs were doing and how life was with their family. May and June were in the kitchen, talking and cooking dinner; as they were talking, June said she saw someone on television say, "American women are tall with long legs, and they have a round head, and most Asian women have short legs and a flat head and flat face." June said, "I think American woman do have long legs and round heads."

When May heard this, she rationalized the explanation of June's behavior. Alarmingly, June's younger brother married an Asian woman and had two children with her. And their son married an American and had a child with her. May could not believe what she was hearing, right then in front of her face, since she came from Asia. May felt some disconnection with civilized social development. Dan had retired from flying airplanes; he had worked with people of many colors, many coworkers of different races—black, white, yellow, or whatever. They all had responsible jobs; therefore, they should be civilized and have an open mind and understand about international marriage. After years of training and schooling, June still lived in the dark, unaware, absentminded, and insensitive. Once again, it went back to her father, Toby.

In March 2010, Joe and Toby had an argument and Toby told Joe to get out of his house. Joe was hurt and stressed that day, and he began to withdraw from the family, and he sought help from Dan and Lake. He called Dan and left a message for his big brother to call him back, but he never did.

Joe was desperate to get help from his big brother, but Dan didn't call until three months later, and then he said, "I am going on vacation with my sons for two weeks; when I come back, we can talk."

"Three months ago, I asked for help, and he just calls now?" Joe could not control his anger.

He calmed down his blood pressure by taking prescription medicine. Three months later, Dan called and said, "Let us go to the bar to talk; we can watch the basketball game and have some dinner while we talk."

Joe asked himself, *What is he saying? How are we going to talk watching basketball in a bar? Basketball games last almost four hours; how could we talk with people in the bar screaming for their team?*

Joe's anger was higher than ever; he said to himself, "I want to talk to Dan about Dad and Lake! I believe that they do not want to talk to me, and Lake is blaming May for having a temper; what does that have to do with May? What does that have to do with May's temper?"

Joe again was disappointed with his brother and sister. Incorrigible, after the things that were going on with the family, they did not trust. At the same time, they do need each other.

Dan had three sons. His oldest son had moved back home and had not worked for almost a year. Soon, his son got a job and moved closer to May and Joe's house. Dan called and said, "We are looking for a place for him to stay that is close to your place."

Joe and May were thinking, after they came to this city, they had not stopped by or said hi in almost five years. Joe had asked Dan for help, but his brother never called him back, and now, they needed help and called to ask for help. The real issue was, they wanted May and Joe to raise their son, to complete the job that they have not finished.

May did not have a problem with watching him; she was just upset with their way of thinking that May should be there when they need it but when Joe needed help, they ignored him with a cold heart. She said, "If they want us to finish the job, then they should ask us to our face and talk to us in person. I can be helpful." May said, "Why are they afraid to talk to me?" But they did not talk to May or Joe. A big brother should watch over a younger brother. "Why didn't they help their young brother?"

How were May and Joe going to help? His brother's son was growing into a young man. If he has not learned from his mother and father, then how was he going to learn from May and Joe?

Once again, the family was having dinner one summer night, back when Kay was only nine years old. Kay was a vivacious, innocent, beautiful young girl. Anyone who visited with May and Joe would pay attention to her.

While visiting with the family, Dan looked at Kay and said to May, "She is going to have four or five children, if not more, and have a different father with every baby!"

May did not understand what Dan was trying to say. And now he wanted May and Joe to finish his job. He could not finish raising a son, but May could. He must have forgotten what he had said to May (or else he was confused). Regardless, that day, Dan did not respect May and innocent Kay.

At the same time, they spoke uncivilly, talking nasty about people of different races that they did not know. When Dan and June were moving to a bigger house, Joe and May came to help them move. Dan's three boys were all growing, yet they were not there to help, but Joe was there to help. They rented a moving truck. As Joe and May were loading boxes into the truck, some friends called Dan to see how he was doing.

He answered, "I have the movers here, and I am all good."

What he was saying to his friend was that May had no experience in moving but she was doing the work herself. The only people helping that day were Joe and May, and she was disabled but trying to lift box after box. And how can a disabled person lift the boxes, how many heavy boxes can she move to the truck?

Dan did not thank Joe and May for being there to help; he called May and Joe "the movers." When May heard that, she thought, "When did I become a mover? My name is May; I am feeling a little defensive because he calls me a mover." May paused for a second and said, "He should have said, 'My sister-in-law and my young brother Joe are helping me, they have driven two hours to be here, and I am thankful they are here to help.'" It was an insult to May and Joe.

May did not hear what he wanted her to hear; she pretended not to hear as he had no thought to family principle. She tried to believe that Dan could be understanding.

With that, every marriage has hardship sometimes. She said, "I do not believe Dan had a perfect marriage; everyone has an argument or disagreement, I prefer not to call names, I thought I knew Dan but I do not know him at all."

Joe, father to two children and May's husband, had done next to nothing to offend Lake and Dan.

Lake and Dan went to college for four years and earned their degrees. Does that mean they are smart? Because they were educated for four years, are they smarter than Joe or May? May did not agree that education made people smart; she said, "If education made them smart, then why doesn't Lake have a job? Instead, she lives in her eighty-nine-year-old father's home and has no place of her own, and Dan is narrow minded; the more I talk to him, the more I get to know him as a bigot."

Dan was out of town almost twenty-five years. June moved

from state to state and raised the children in different military communities. They moved every five years. He saw people of all colors, and his children learned from them all.

"Where has he been?" May said to Joe. "Life is a journey, sometimes, the journey is schooling, we must teach children and give them a formal education. The child going to school is most critical, but parents must educate their children, it's another way to make the child a productive member of society." May said again and again, "You thought you could trust your family, it was the most vital to trust!"

Dan moved back home after his children had grown up. For twenty-five years he did not see what was going on with Toby and Sue and Lake and Joe. Twenty-five years is a long time. He did not see but rather heard by word of mouth and thought that's what happened. He did not help when his young brother needed to be helped, nor did Lake. Instead, when Lake needed help moving, Joe and May were there to help. How many times did she move? The number of times was unknown, too many. When Dan needed help, Joe and May were there to help move and more. But Dan never called to ask how he was doing; if he called, it was because Dan needed something from Joe or his children needed May's children to keep them company. Or Dan liked to show off in front of his children that he was the number one son. Standing tall as Dan, grandfather to seven grandchildren and one great-grandchild, Toby was father to three children. Toby saw Dan's pride and wanted to help Dan; he chose Dan over Joe, pointing at Joe and saying, "This dumb trucker was speeding and honking to some @#@# n— women; I could not believe what I saw!"

Joe was humiliated by Toby in front of all the family; most of all, he was humiliated in front of Otto and Kay.

It was unthinkable to May, who said, "What kind of education is that for children and grandchildren?"

That is not a healthy family to be around. With Toby's actions, Kay saw and heard; she began to be scared of her grandfather. One day she had a complex going on and Kay said, "Mommy, I do not like what Grandfather said the other day, calling Dad a dumb trucker; I do not want to go there!"

May said to Kay, "You do not have to go there if you do not like what he says, and we will not go there, okay, Kay? I love you for caring, that is a good feeling." May said again and again that someone should hear about Toby's abuse and get this family help. That day, Toby was humiliated in front of all the family; Dan was the highlight of the family because Toby chose him over Joe.

May saw Dan across the table, smiling with beaming eyes, pleased with himself because his father put down his brother Joe. May could feel the big brother's elation, at the same time, she did not trust in the brother-to-brother relationship. The bond between father and son was nothing but quackery. As far as other family members, Joe told May about the teacher who called him an evil name because he was left handed and whipped him with a yard stick. That teacher was June's grandmother.

Joe was always watching himself, thinking that he was not bright and had a learning problem. Joe had to work two or three times harder to survive. He became a narcissist, with excessive interest in himself. Specifically, he did not want to work with his children; he had no interest in being a father.

That is to say, in his childhood, he had no help from Toby or Dan or Lake. What he saw was what he did. In other words, Joe saw what Toby did, and he became like his father. He did not help his children do their homework, and he did not pay attention to them either. May had to give attention to both children, but a father's attention and a mother's attention are two different kinds of love. Mothers cannot give a child a father's love, and fathers cannot give a child a mother's love. Otto needed his father to play football with him. Instead of May playing football, she played Asian games with Otto like BODOOGI or KOORDE. She did not know how to play football. In Asia, many students played soccer or were cheerleaders in school. At the same time, May tried to help them do their homework; doing a father and mother's job was not easy.

May said, "Single mothers and single fathers should be honored; it is the most rewarding job. We should all give them respect and reward single parents." May made these comments about single parents because she felt like one; she was doing all the homework and helping Otto grow into a man by being a housewife and going to work and become a corporate leader. It was a heavy burden for one woman.

It was an endless job; one day, May came home from work, and Joe had been fired from his job. Joe was fired from many jobs. At that time, May was going to school for accounting and working as an AP clerk; she was mother to two children without help from her husband or his family, and she fought many days to help her children grow and stay away from drugs. She thought that Joe could work harder to provide for them, but he did not. He was home almost six months without a job. He fed himself cheese sandwiches. As nourishing as cheese was, Otto and Kay did not like to eat cheese.

Six months later, May had to drop her class; she thought she could take one semester off and go back to finish up, but she did not make it. It was hard on her job and her family. May found that life was not perfect. The life she had was full of privation. She no longer loved Joe. That feeling was broken when she arrived in Chicago Airport, carrying her son. Now she felt that she had to stand as firmly on her two feet as she could.

Later, May learned that Joe was not a leader; May had to help him look for a job. She told Joe where he should go to look for a job.

May had no job training and did not have any work skills. She had no support and did not know who she needed to ask. The only thing she knew was to keep her eyes and ears open, to give a thought to living.

Joe was not the cleanest person. He did not like to take a shower or brush his teeth. May helped the children stay healthy by brushing their teeth and eating well. Joe always liked to cook for himself and May. But he did not cook for the children. He liked to eat American food, which can feed one's hunger for a little amount of money. He learned that from Sue, spending time in the kitchen with his mother, learning how to cook pies and more.

However, May had to say, he was not the cleanest person, and without a clean person to cook, there are a lot of issues like food poisoning. May had a problem because eating the food he cooked was making her sick. When she found that he was not a clean person, May no longer let him cook in the kitchen. Most of all, he was insecure and jealous. He learned from Toby that marriage is abuse.

May remembered years ago when she was young and did not know what Joe's young life was like. But May wanted to have a child. She was young and hard-headed, skinny as a chopstick, a ninety-five-pound girl who was not thinking clearly, all she had in her mind was getting far from her home. She thought having a son would make all her problems go away.

Joe just wanted to have fun, he did not want to have a child at that time. His personality started to show an evil side. May had no idea where he was going. May had no work experience and did not know where her money would come from. One thing May had in mind: Joe needed to work to bring income for the family. When May came to America, she brought money from Korea; it was not much, but enough to make a down payment on a house.

Later, Toby asked Joe for money to pay for phone calls overseas.

May could not understand and asked, "Why do we have to give money to your parents?" He explained, "When I was overseas, phone calls were not cheap; they are asking me to help pay the phone bills, and I think we should."

She understood, but at the same time, it was not clear that the phone bill was over $500! She had no time to argue. And she went along with Joe and gave him money to pay off the phone bill.

The storm passed, he was laid off from his job and got another job, and he said to May, "I have not saved money right now, but when I retire, I will get Social Security from the government."

May did not know what Social Security was or why the government would give him money. May did not know what would happen but she believed that Joe would take care of her and their child. May learned what Social Security was, but she later asked Joe, "If I do not have any work, then how is the government going to pay me Social Security?"

Joe had no answer, then he said to May, "When I die, you are going to receive some money from that!" May had to believe that, but her mind was always thinking that he was not telling the full truth. She had to remind herself to watch out for that family. Once again, he had no interaction with the children; he did not help with their activities and made no internal connection with them. Her two children had no father; no discipline was taken against them. Otto and Kay needed attention from their father's mental and moral direction; all children need that from their father. At the same time, he behaved like a child. If he needed attention from May, then he was as nice as could be.

After he got what he wanted out of May, he was like another person. He had a problem with abuse like Toby, yelling and acting like a child, slamming the door and going out to the garage. May thought about her stepfather; he would clean the house and knew how to take care of children. She may not have been a good child all the time, but she knew that; that was then and this was the time to be responsible; she had an obligation to show authority to her children without help.

Many times, Joe would ask May to go to supermarket for bread and milk and so on. Before going to supermarket, he always asked her to make him lunch. May tried to save money, save every penny, but Joe liked to spend money, and he was a big eater. Joe ordered ham, gravy with biscuits, eggs, toast, and a drink. It could feed almost five people, but it did not matter. After he ate, he was ready to go to the supermarket; as he drove, he started complaining about Otto and Kay, who May loved dearly.

He started to complain about how Otto and Kay did this and did that; he did not want his son to play with his tools. May told Joe, "You are the father! Why don't you tell Otto not to play with your tools? If you do, why can't he?"

He began to have problems with the children.

May told him, "You do not complain about Otto and Kay, they have been doing good and you need to give attention to those children as their father figure. Do not ever complain about my children again!" May screamed and called him names, saying, "You just no-good father @#@#, and no good @#@# husband!"

He learned that it was not a good idea to complain to May, because she would scream and yell. May was asking for help, but Joe had no response.

Food had to be on the dinner table every day, every week, and every year before the children grew up and moved away from home and made a place of their own. May did not know how cook. She only learned how to cook from cooking in high school. The first time May cooked rice, she burned it; it was not edible. The first time she cooked a hamburger on the top of the stove, it looked like a big meatball.

May was thinking, *How can Joe eat that hamburger? Love must make him blind.* When May went to the supermarket and saw a pizza, she said, "That plate of bread with a layer of noodles looks good; can I try that?"

Joe heard and snickered to himself; he did not bother to explain— he just bought the pizza. Later, May found that the top of the pizza was not noodles but cheese. There were many things May had to learn for herself, and she made many mistakes. She always tried to fix whatever she could. May went to the supermarket every week, and Joe went with her. Joe liked ham and canned goods, and that's what he wanted to eat. May learned how to clip coupons and save money. He liked a big ham and wanted to have one. May did not think they needed such a big ham and tried to buy a smaller one. Joe did not like the smaller ham; he asked for the big ham.

May asked Joe, "Why do we need that big ham? Why do we have to have that big ham?"

Joe did not like what May said, and he became cantankerous and angry in front of the crowd, saying to May, "What is the matter with that ham?" Joe yelled as he walked along pushing the shopping cart.

May heard Joe; she did not know how to take his unmanly, contemptible reaction. May had a problem with Joe for a long time, but she did not think he would have such an endless temper and make matters so difficult. Sometimes, she argued with him in the supermarket. May learned not to take Joe shopping with her, but he would beg and plead, saying, "I will try not to argue with you, can I go with you, please?"

May gave Joe another chance and took him with her, but he did not know how to behave like a man. May said to him, "Please be a man and try not to act like a big bully in front of the crowd like your father. I do not accept that, and you degrade me in front of other people. I feel hurt when you do that." May asked him to stop. But Joe did it again and again.

She knew he needed to go see a counselor. May went herself and asked for help from a counselor; she said, "I do not feel Joe loves me or the children, and I feel used by him for what he needs himself, he is not with me or not for children."

The counselor asked May, "Why do you feel he does not love you and your children?"

She answered, "When we visit his parents, he ignores the children, he does not fix plates for Otto and Kay, he stays away when the children need attention from their dad, and he fixes the best for himself and more."

May asked Joe many times for help. Later, the counselor told May, "Your husband is not going to give you what you need, he is not going to work harder like you ask. He does not want the children you have with him, you wanted to have children. He is not going to give you any attention, he is thinking you just want attention from him. For all that, you must leave him if you are better off without him. Most of all, your husband tells me you have to work to get what you need."

When May heard what the counselor said, she was hurt but she had a feeling her future with Joe was not promising. At that time, May was young and hard-headed; she learned there was a difference between Asians, Europeans, and Americans. May believed in marriage but this was not what she had in mind; her husband did not act the way she wanted. People in a marriage should work together, husbands and wives should respect each other and share the life they promise. But May had learned about her journey in school, she went along and tried to stand on her own two feet. May tried as hard as she could. The children were married and had their own houses and careers; they advanced through life after moving out. Their mom's job was done and they moved on to their next journey.

But May's journey was not over; her adventure with Joe began to show problems; they could not work out their relationship as husband and wife. After years of stress, May had a heart problem, and she had a mild heart attack. She needed to stay home to take care of herself. She walked five miles a day and brought down her weight. After eating all that fried chicken and mashed potatoes and pies that had sugar and butter, in no time her 95 pounds came to be 110 pounds, and after her second child came along, she became 125 pounds. Then, after sitting in an office working all day in front of a computer, her weight grew to 135 pounds. In no time, the children had moved out, and in a blink of an eye, her weight went to 150 and then to 170 pounds. She did not like looking at herself in the mirror.

As she worked every day, she brought back her positive spirit. She stayed home, thinking about working things out with Joe. Joe was not learning; he was thinking of all the attention she gave to the children. Now he thought it was time for her to give him attention. He called May every day while she was at work.

If she had to work overtime, he would call May and ask, "Where are you? I have been sitting in this little room for almost two hours, and this worker knows I have been waiting, yet he does not care; he looks past me and ignores me!"

May could not take his complaints but she had to calm him down; she said, "Okay, I hear you, but you need to calm down and sit back and read a book or go out for a walk; after all, we need the extra money."

Joe would calm down, and when she came home, he demanded attention. Joe liked May's cooking. Joe was looking for May to cook for him and serve him, and May thought that Joe should do it himself. Again, where she came from, the husband would bring home the income and wife would stay home and take care of the family.

She had no rule of thumb; she cooked and Joe fixed himself a plate and sat on the recliner, eating while watching TV, commenting on someone he saw, saying, "What is the matter with him? Look at his nose; his nose is way too big!"

May looked at him and said, "Look at yourself. You do not have good-looking body; you know how fat you got? Do not talk about others!"

Every day he would sit in front of the TV, eating and drinking sugary iced tea, acting like his father, complaining and complaining. With every bit of food in his mouth, his breath would smell and May would smell rotten food and fat cells from meat.

May could not take it, she had enough. On weekends, Joe would stay home most of the time; she might ask him to do some work, but he did not care and would say to her, "I will do that tomorrow." But tomorrow would become next week, and then next month, and then months would go by. May made many mistakes. She often told her children how she was blind, that she did not see how he was living.

One hot day in the summer, she and Joe went to an ice cream shop. Joe thought he'd take May take out and have some fun with Otto. Joe was getting two scoops of ice cream, and May saw the young girl working at the shop; she must have been around sixteen. May thought something was the matter with the young girl; she was overweight or obese. Overseas, a "fat cat" is a wealthy person who eats well. Yet May thought this girl was too young to be wealthy; she wondered why she was overweight, and she felt sorry for her and wanted to help.

May asked that young lady, "Are you okay? Why are you fat? Can I help you?"

Joe wondered what she was thinking. He got mad and screamed at May, "Stop talking! Get into the car!" Joe paid the overweight young lady with additional money and said, "I am so sorry about what my wife said; she will not say it again to you."

Then the overweight young lady told Joe, "It is okay; I have heard that many times, and I am used to that kind of comment from all kinds of people. Thank you again for being kind."

Joe rushed into the car like a mad dog. May did not know that what she said to that overweight young lady was wrong. May was scared and did not know what to say to Joe. Joe drove home and took her into the living room; he told May with a calm voice, "In America, we do not ask a person why they are fat! You don't say again to any other person, 'Why you are fat?' Do you understand that?"

May heard and understood that she had made a mistake. She said to Joe, "I am sorry; I will not say it again, but I am still wondering why she was fat. Can you explain it to me? I would like to learn more about things going on around here; overseas, you do not see overweight people like here. Can you explain, please?"

Joe could not explain; he said, "I have no idea why. Just do not say it again!"

"Okay, I will not say it again."

When May looked back on that day, she said, "I am so sorry that I called her fat; I will not ever say that word to another person. Look at myself; I am so fat and overweight. I hope to see her again and apologize."

May looked at herself and understood; she said, "I know why people become overweight; look at me—I am overweight. Look at my American family—most of them are overweight."

Joe did not want May to slim down. He liked to see her overweight like other women who stayed home. He would not say it to her, but May thought Joe wanted her to be overweight. If Joe lost May or she left him, then he would lose his manhood. He would not find another woman as good as May, and he told her, "We are going to be together for eternity; do not forget that." Joe told May this again and again, but May looked at him and said, "You are out of your mind and ridiculous, unbalanced, and the most obsessed man I have ever seen." Joe could not lose May.

May thought that positive thinking would help in life. She learned from school and from her mother that a smile will brighten your day. May did not like to be negative.

May liked to be happy, but Joe did not like when she was laughing. Joe would say, "Okay, you are laughing too much; stop laughing!"

May would look at Joe and ask, "What is the matter? You do not like my happiness? If you do not like that I am happy, then you can cry yourself!"

Joe started crying himself; he was trying to take a nap in the living room. As soon as he lay down on the couch, he snored so loud May wanted to close her ears. While he was taking nap, May decided to do some laundry. After she hung up his pants and shirts, she went into the kitchen to see what to make for dinner. As she passed through the living room, she thought she heard him snoring, but as she passed by, she glanced at him with the corner of her eye and saw him peeking out of his eye, mocking May.

May thought, *Did I see his eyes? He was not sleeping a second ago, but now he is snoring like he has been sleeping for some time. I might be mistaken. How can he change in second?*

May tried again; she passed in front of Joe, carrying the laundry basket into another room and looking at him again. Again his eyes were peeking and following where May went. Joe was mocking her all these years, watching where she was going, what she was doing, even what she ate. Then Joe complained and complained.

One day, May was mad at her lazy, fat, mocking husband and told him, "I know your eyes are following me where I go. You are not taking a nap, and you are not tired; you're just being lazy. You do not like me to be happy; you are mocking me. If I want to do something nice, you do not like what I am doing, and you do not like saving money because you do not want your children to have money. You are lazy because you do not want the children to have a happy life; get out!"

Of course, Joe got up and looked at May, saying, "Cheer up, okay? I was not mocking you, I was just looking at what you were doing; that is all, okay? Cheer up."

Joe got up and went outside. It took May a long time to find out what kind of husband he was; May could not get out of the relationship she created. Joe was not going to let go of her. Where was May going to be in the future? One day on the news, they were talking about Social Security. He heard and said to May, "I do not have a problem with what we have. I am okay with what money I am making. I am not going to work when I am sixty-one years old; what I have is good. When I retire from this job, I'll have money coming from Social Security and the union; I should be okay."

Again May heard him talking about going to be okay, because he had money coming from Social Security when he retired. May asked him, "It is good, but where will money come from when I retire at age sixty-five?"

He looked at her and his face became red. "The money I have coming is yours too."

"No way—you're trying to tell me that Social Security money is mine?" May had to think hard and reorganize her life, since her

Social Security money was not enough to retire on. When she retired, the Social Security money was not something May could rely on.

One time when May came home, Joe said, "Ask your brother to help us with some money."

May looked at him and thought, Am I really hearing this? Why is he telling me to ask my brother to give him some money? She could not understand what he was trying to ask.

May had to get up and work as an AP clerk for an accounting firm, and she was going to school for a degree and trying to raise two young children while she was in school. Every morning, she would get up at five o'clock. She showered and dried her hair; then Kay took a shower, and then Otto would get up and they were ready to go to school and May would go to work.

All that time, did he help? What did he do? May was overworked; at the same time, Joe stayed home cooking whatever he wanted to eat, feeding himself. He just watched movies or cartoons on TV all day and every night.

One day, they were visiting his parents, and Sue asked Joe how his family was doing.

Joe answered, "Every morning the hair dryer goes on like a jet passing, and the loud noise wakes me up. Every day!" Dan and Lake looked at May; she thought, *He is complaining about us!* That was not all; he said, "And every day she walks with high heel shoes making noise like a school teacher coming down the hall!"

When May heard this, she looked at Joe and said, "I did not know you felt like I am a schoolteacher coming down the hall every day; we will talk when we get home."

The family was quiet and acted like they did not hear Joe. That day May was done with Joe; she said to him, "I cannot believe what I heard today. If you do not like what I am doing to provide for this family, then get out! I do not need you!"

Joe pleaded with May to forgive him; he knew that what he said was wrong. "Please forgive me, I will never do it again or say that again!"

She said, "Don't you ever complain about my children, Kay and Otto, again; do you understand that, you F##@#!"

That day May saw another person in Joe. She had no one to talk to and nowhere to go for help. May would get up in the morning, dry her hair, put on high-heel shoes, and go to work.

Regarding the lives of Kay and Otto, their futures were bright. Even though Joe did none of the work to raise them, he would look at them and say, "We did it." What was he trying to tell May: we, we, and we? He did not help the children when they needed help, he did not give them attention when they needed a father's attention, he did not help with their homework, he did not fix them dinner, he ignored them. Where did he get the idea that "we" did it?

Joe let May do all the work, and now he wanted to be in with her and say, "We did it." Please. May heard again and again from Joe; one day, Dan told Joe, "I am so jealous of your children, I am still helping my children financially." Joe heard his brother's remarks, which became a big deal to the family. Otto and Kay stayed in their jobs and had their own place to stay and paid their bills. Joe still complained about Otto and Kay; May had been arguing with him, defending the children, others were criticizing her children, but May would not stop helping Otto and Kay. May said, "It is a parent's job to help their children, they are their guardian, they keep them safe, shielded, children should feel they can go to them when they child have a problem, and show that they are here to help and protect them."

But Joe told May, "Dan does not have to help his children, who says we have to help our children?"

May reminded Joe that he had no help from Toby, but Joe helped Toby and Sue. When Joe came home from Army camp, he often brought them food and money. On the contrary, May could see that his mom and dad were unkind and bitter, but when you grow up and have children of your own, you should be accountable to the children you bring into this wicked world.

May heard Joe's unkind, cold-hearted thoughts about Otto and Kay; she said, "If I have money to help my children, I will help them. Children are educated in school, but it is so important that they become individuals; Otto and Kay might have moved out and have their own place to stay, but they still need a mother and father's love when they are stressed about their job; they look for someone to talk to, their parents should be there to hear them no matter what their age."

Joe had nothing to say to May. He believed that every child should work and earn their own money. He had no help and did not save for the future. If Joe had $10 in his pocket, he would act like he had $100; $10 worth of food became $100 worth of food in the shopping cart. He was not good in math; he did not know where his money went. He wanted to buy things he did not need. Or he would buy something that was overpriced, thinking that because it cost a lot, it was good.

May argued with him about finances; Joe had the mind of a child, he was not farsighted or prudent. May had no medical insurance for now, but did her husband care? Instead, he asked May to stay home. May knew she needed to work, but she said to Joe, "You think I should stay home cooking dinner for you every day and take care of you every day? I would not mind staying home if we had enough money to do things, but how are we going to do

things without money? If I am sick, how are you going to pay?"
Joe had no answer.

May was wise about the world and intellectual matters. She said,
"He is not a smart man, all the time I have been with him, he
was thinking about when he retires, how to save money so that
he could have it, and he would be free, emotionally, mentally, and
physically, and he'd sit back and let May do all the work. When
the time comes, he says 'We did it,' but there was never 'we'!"

As for dreams and attention, May never gave up her dreams; she
was trying to create her future with her own business.

Sue spoke softly and had low self-esteem. May had never seen Sue
raise her voice. At the same time, she had cooking experience that
she learned from her mother. She canned all the veggies and some
meat. May had no idea what to cook for dinner; when cooking
Thanksgiving dinner, she had no idea how to cook a turkey, or
what to make at other times. Sue also made her own wedding
dress and knitted. Sue always liked to visit with May. When May
visited, Sue would show her how to can the veggies. Sometimes,
she cooked in front of May; she taught her how to bake an apple
pie, cakes, and cookies.

Sue bonded with May; she spent time teaching her whenever she
could. All that time, May did not know that bonding with her
would bring her closer to Kay. Even thinking back, May had no
interaction with Kim, her mother, who was busy bringing in the
money and running the businesses. Her mother took care of her
three brothers and a sister whose husband died in the Korean War.
Kim helped all the nephews and nieces, and she put them through
college. Kim did not have time to show May how to cook. She
would make excuses, "We are going to do it tonight when I come
home from a business meeting, okay, May?" But the meeting went
too long and she could not make it; it was too late to cook.

May spent a lot of time with Sue. Sue tested how smart May was.

Toby was trying to show how life insurance could save them some money; May wrote down how much money could accumulate over the years. Toby looked at all the numbers quickly and said to Joe, "This girl has some math skills."

It was the first test, and Sue trying to show, but May had learned some skills from Kim, like knitting, it was not hard to do. Yet May had no complaints, she was eager to learn from Sue.

One day, May was visiting Sue, and they were bonding; Sue showed May how to make homemade noodles. Sue poured bleached white flour into a bowl made of clay; it must have been her favorite bowl, and she had used it many times. It had some chips and the bowl's color was faded way, which showed she had used it many times. She cracked some eggs into the clay bowl with flour and some salt.

She mixed it with her hand and asked May, "Would you like to mix this flour?"

May was happy that Sue asked that; she said, "Okay, I'd be glad to do it." May took over the mixing bowl, trying to mix with her hand. That was the first time she made noodles with Sue. It was the first time May had the feeling of wet flour in her hands. May had no idea what wet flour can do, making pie dough and cakes and more. She had no cooking experience from overseas. Kim always had a helper or hired a cook.

May was excited and thrilled to help Sue, but most of all she was glad to learn how to make homemade noodles. She had no idea how to make homemade noodles. Next, May learned how to cut the noodles. Learning how to make homemade noodles that day stayed in her mind; she makes them every year. When cold winter comes, May remembers making homemade noodles with Sue. Every time she cooks homemade noodles, she remembers being in the kitchen, with wet flour on her hands, laughing, and the dry flour was all over the counter top. It was a good time and an innocent time, it comforted her, and Joe and Otto liked to eat the noodles and asked for more.

Every time May visited Sue in the hospital, she brought homemade noodles. Sue was happy to eat the homemade noodles and bragged about the noodles May made. After she ate the noodles, she was comfortable and took a nap, pleased that she had homemade noodles.

Looking back, May thought about all the bonding she did with Sue, learning many things; she wondered, "Why didn't Lake learn how to make homemade noodles? And June could bake sweet cookies of any kind and can cook with flour, but she did not know how to make homemade noodles."

May did not understand that the family was missing out on mother and daughter bonding. As she learned how to make homemade noodles, she thought, *I must show Otto and Kay how good Sue was, and I hope to teach them how to make homemade noodles. Some day, they are going to remember those good things.*

Sue also liked sewing and knitting. Every time she visited with May, she would show her how to sew, knit, or cook. They might have had cultural differences, but their mother-to-daughter interaction was the same. The love between a mother and daughter was a lifetime treasure. May learned and she taught Kay how to shop and save money for the future. Kay worked since the tender age of fifteen. May could not buy things with her income, but she knew how to save and stretch one dollar into one hundred dollars. May and Kay had no time to cook or bake cookies, but they interacted by shopping smart and saving money in the bank. May and Kay always shopped at Goodwill stores and always looked for sales.

May say to Kay, "Do not buy anything that is not on sale; always look for sales." With mother and daughter bonding, May and Kay would talk about how much money she can save. May was proud to spend time with Kay, giving her a lifetime treasure; Kay learned from her mother and grandmother. May did not learn how to make cookies, but she knew how to make homemade applesauce that was out of this world. Otto and Kay would ask for her homemade applesauce every year. They also asked for her homemade noodles when they came for Thanksgiving dinner. Dan and Lake had no homemade noodles on Thanksgiving. It was sad, deplorable, and disheartening.

When children move out from home, whether their parents helped or not, the children are not owed anything by their parents. Nor do the parents owe anything to their children. After one moves out, it is a hardship without getting help from one's mother and father. Away from family, wishing to be closer to family, is part of being a parent. Good times and bad times, everyone of us has hardships and good times, but where do children go to ask for help? Most children ask their parents. Recall, Joe had been helped himself. Parents plant the seeds, and they pass on the hope in the future to their grandchildren. No matter what the child becomes, tall, short, fat, dumb, or smart, the child comes from part of the father and grow in their mother's womb, and then they are born into a world they did not ask to born into.

May said, "You brought a child into the world, then that is the parents' problem, not the child's. Parents must pay attention to their child, help them to grow and learn right from wrong and choose their future life."

May's journey continued: teaching Otto and Kay to become a young man and lady. Laughing and crying, May learned how to be a good mother to her children. There was no regret or hesitating to be a courageous, great warrior for this country, an outstanding achievement in life. May helped Otto and Kay become good citizens to this community and country; they became young adults, and their friends looked at Otto and Kay as proud to be their friends.

May said, "Being a mother, you do anything to help your child grow, and they learn to speak and act as leaders, providing good reflection to the next generation. No matter what color or what ethnicity, Otto and Kay are the future."

May was clear, she did not give up to petty people who tried to push her around, like Toby, a self-seeking, overbearing, arrogant father and grandfather. First, she was glad to learn how to cook homemade noodles and bond with Joe's mother and Otto's grandmother. Regardless of whether Lake cared or not, she did not know how to make homemade noodles and missed out on bonding and sharing feelings with her mother; it could have been the highlight of a vivid education to every grandchild. May thought that teaching Otto and Kay how to make homemade noodles would help them enjoy Thanksgiving dinner and carry on the hope and love of the future.

CHAPTER 21
The Letters

Thinking back to when Joe and May moved to the city, Joe was fired from many jobs. For that reason, May had go to work, and she had no choice, she had to do it. If not, the children, Otto and Kay, would starve. She had no job experience, no skills, and no job training. She tried anything to get a job and provide food on the table and feed the children. One time, both Joe and May had jobs. Two paychecks were nice to have, providing food and things the young children needed. Toby did not like that May had a job and they were bringing two paychecks for Joe's family. Toby was jealous, possessive, and envious because May had a job and was helping Joe financially.

Toby's envy made him write a letter to Joe; the letter said, "Dear son, I hope that you are aware that we helped May when she came to America. Your mother and I picked her up from the airport and she lived with us; all those years we helped you two folks, we have the documentation that we spent $40,000, which helped you buy your first house and get a job with Mayflower, and free automobiles, and we gave money to Otto and Kay when they graduated from high school, and more."

May could not read Toby's handwriting; it looked like it had been written by a first grader. May asked Joe, "Can you read this?"

Then Joe picked up the letter and tried to make sense of it, taking it one word at a time.

May said, "Yes, Toby and Sue did pick me up from the airport, I am thankful for that, but the rest is a lie. When I came to America, I brought money with me, thirty-five years ago $3,500 was a lot of money, that money was the down payment on our first house, I helped you get your job with Mayflower, I bought the automobiles, I had a job and bought them cheap, we paid with cash, and the money he gave to Otto and Kay was to celebrate them graduating from high school. I cannot say Toby did not help us, but fathers help their children, it is being a parent, and parents do help their children."

All those years, Toby helped Lake move and helped raise her children. She still lived with Toby, rent free and with free food.

Lake's son Junk lived with Toby for many years. May said, "He would take him to work and bring him back to his house and feed him; most of the time he did not have a job but he was living rent free; did he document all that?"

Joe stopped for a second and then said, "My father helped Junk get married and gave him money to buy a house and bought him a truck and a car, which he wrecked. He took him to Florida, and he stayed in Florida, and every weekend, Lake goes to Toby's house, the babysitting was free, I cannot count all the many things my father helped my sister with, my father helped her to finish beauty school and more!"

Joe was mad and wondered how to answer the letter himself; he called Lake and said, "Hi Lake. I received a letter from Dad saying that I owed him $40,000. Did you receive a letter from him?"

Lake said, "No, he never said anything to me, and I did not get a letter from him. I do not understand, why did he send a letter to you?"

Joe was lost, and most of all, May did not understand; she asked, "Where did he get all these lies from?"

Then Joe said to May, "When I was in the Army, many times I bought food from the military supermarket, canned goods, meat, and more, because it saved money, 50 percent, and I gave money to Mom when I came home to visit. I trusted Mom and sent her money to save for me, but later I found that my Toby lost his job and they had to pay the bills with the money I sent. When I came home there was no money, but we did help them when I came home. I asked you to pay the phone bill and food, do you remember?"

May's memory was clear as it could be; she said, "Yes I do, I gave you money and asked why we had to give your parents money."

This was not the only time Toby wrote letter to Joe saying that May and Joe owed him money. The second letter made Joe madder than ever. It said, "Dear family, I am writing this letter to thank Lake, June, and Dan for all the help I received from them. When we moved, it was hot and we did lots of walking. At this time, I am adjusting, and we are happy with our new home. We are unpacking kitchen boxes. Your mom is cooking our first meal, fried chicken and fried potatoes. We are glad we bought this house, we call it our new home. It is not as big as the house we had, but it is what I have been looking for all my life. And I am writing to thank Lake, June, and Dan for all the help from you guys. Again, thank you for all the help. Good old Dad."

Joe read the letter and grew hot-tempered, confused, and distracted, saying with an angry voice, "What is the matter with him? Who was there when he was moving five times, every move? Big brother was not there to help, or Lake. Who helped them find a house? Lake helped them find a house, because she needed a babysitter for free while she went out looking for a man every week, which

Mom and Dad are doing this moment, babysitting their great-grandchild, every week. He's saying I have not helped!"

May wondered why he was as mad as a dog. She asked with a calming voice, "Please explain to me, why did this letter make you that mad?"

May read it and discovered that Joe's name was not on the thank-you letter. He looked at his wife and said, "Now you understand why I am angry!"

She was no longer confused and said, "I could see your anger, but I am not surprised; knowing your dad, it could be he forgot to write your name, but how can a father forget his son?"

Joe got madder and madder; he said, "You know when my uncle died, Lake's ex-husband was there to help my aunt. While he was helping her, he stole money from my aunt."

May did not know about this; she asked, "How did he do that?"

Joe did not want to talk about it, but he needed to tell the truth; he explained to May, "Every time he was visiting and it looked like he was helping, he was writing checks to himself. Sue told me he took a lot of money, but that is not all; before my aunt died, she had to sell her house and go to a care center. She did not have children and the house was paid off, and she put the house up for sale before she moved out. All the things she had were sold; most of them were worthless, but where did all the money go? And she had a ring that was worth a lot of money. The dining table went to Lake's daughter; many other things were gone overnight. At that time, Lake was helping our aunt, yet you and I went to help her move and cleaned the house before she went into the nursing home. How sad it was! And my F#$#$#$ father could not see, if not he was that ignorant; the house he moved to is all about Lake wanting to have him around, so she can use Mom and Dad again and again. My father is thoughtless."

Joe might say that his father was not a smart person, but May did not think Toby was thoughtless.

Every time he invited Junk to visit, Toby used him as he pleased. Junk worked on Toby's garden, built his back porch, and mowed the lawn, but at the same time, Junk used Toby for free rent, free dinner, most of all he was lazy. Junk did not try hard in his life; he got a free ride to work, Toby had to get up and take him to work and pick him up, even on snowy and cold days. People asked, "Why does Toby have to get up and remove snow from the driveway so he can take his grandson to work? Why doesn't Junk get up a little early and remove the snow himself? Toby is almost ninety years old, Junk is forty. Please give him some credit, he was not a good father or grandfather, but he is trying in his old age."

Toby wrote many letters to Joe that were hurtful. Toby wrote many times about his living will, which he changed many times. Joe received the last before Sue passed away. It was not known who decided whose names were in the will. For a child to see their name would be hurtful and a disgrace, inviting distrust. That you know, but yet you did not know, your parents as well as siblings. In a living will declaration, Joe looked for his name, but he could not find it. Lake and Dan's names were in the will. What happened was the day Toby wrote the will, he took out Joe's name.

Joe's face started to get red, soon he was screaming, "So I am not my father's son! I am nothing to him, I am just a dumb trucker. What have I done that my father does not know my name? He has robbed me of my life's dream." Joe paused a moment and took a deep breath; his voice went up again and he said, "I have helped that man many times; when he got laid off work, I gave him money to put food on the table; every time he moved, I was there to help; what does he want from me? When I was stationed overseas, I sent home money in my name, but they paid bills with my money. He is a thief, he robbed my life with a thieving mentality, and he is deplorable. I cannot stand him; if there were no law, I might kill him."

May could not say anything; she just looked at him and tried to calm him down. She rubbed his back kindly and tenderly; she said, "What have you done? I do not know why your dad didn't put your name in the will; your anger will not help you get what you want from your dad. You need to calm down and think about what to do."

Joe calmed down, but May could feel he needed an answer from that letter. When he did not hear from his father, he got a phone call from Dan, who said, "I received a letter from Dad about the living will, and I am going to send a copy to you."

Joe was thinking, "You received the living will declaration?" Joe had not received it yet, and he made Dan believe that he was expecting to get the same letter from their dad. Dan knew Joe had not gotten a letter from Toby. Joe waited almost a year and six months, and then Dan called and said, "Your name is on the living will, and I will send it to you."

Joe said, "You are telling me, my name is on the living will?"

Dan repeated, "Yes, your name is on the living will."

Both brothers were playing. Joe did not let Dan know that he did not get a letter with the living will from Toby, but he also never got a letter from Dan.

"Where is the letter?" he asked his wife.

May had no answer; she said, "You just have to wait, I suppose."

Dan was known for always delaying. People said he would be late for his own funeral. Sue would tease Dan for being slow, for ignoring the family during get-togethers, for being slow in many other ways. Therefore, he might delay delivering something like an important letter; it might not be important to Dan, but it was important to Joe; it might give him some hope and show he was accepted by Toby and loved by the family. Yet Dan could not see that Joe was mistrusted, and he misunderstand who Joe was. Even Lake did not try to understand the young brother's feelings or thoughts.

Joe said to May, "It does not matter right now, it does not matter at this moment, I only care about my family, and my father is gone in my spirit. It has been a long time since I was born. I have no desire to return to my family."

May said to Joe, "You might say that to me right now, but I do not believe that it is going to be happen. It does not matter, but at this moment, I think you do love your family."

CHAPTER 22
Going Back Home (Overseas)

Going back home was a dream for May, like the stars of destiny. But going home would please May's family and her mother, Kim, asking for forgiveness for her pains all these years. And the heart has its reasons, which it does not know. The journey was an education to May. She remembered going camping at a monastery. Every summer, Kim took her to see the monks at a monastery, where she could learn to behave like a young lady. At the same time, May was scared to go home. She thought Kim might put May into the monastery or send her to a woman's jail house; knowing May herself, it had been a lifelong drama and an emotional event that helped her over the years become as good as she could be.

Yet May knew that a grown woman does not scare and will not be scared off. She said, "I am not going to let her control me, I am a grown woman." She thought she could be herself, be strong, and stand by herself. "This time, I will not run away from anybody. I will say what's been on my mind all these years. I could not tell my mother before, but this time I will."

Going back home was mentally and emotionally challenging. May thought, "I am not sure it is a good idea; should I go home?" The most scary question of all was, "Will I make it back to America again and see my children?"

It was a scary thought; it brought her back to when she left Korea while she was carrying Otto. It had been a long time since she left her home country. That time, she was a young and hard-headed girl, skinny as a chopstick, an immature young woman who thought she knew it all. She had dreams that she thought she could achieve but she did not know how. Now May had plumped up; she was overweight, 130 pounds; back then, she weighed 95 pounds.

Peeking out the airplane window, she could not believe it. The city was filled with skyscrapers; the buildings were taller than they were twenty-five years ago. She thought, "I feel like I am in Chicago, yet I am in Korea this time."

In no time, the plane touched down. Walking off the plane with the crowd, May had a lump in her throat, and tears were coming down her cheeks; she wiped them off with her hand, trying not to show emotional stress. People were rushing to meet their family and friends waiting at the front of the gate, and May was looking for her mother, Kim. Soon, she saw Aunt Kim and big brother Kim, who were waiting for May and were pleased to see her.

May was a little hesitant with uncertainty; she said to herself, "Where is my Mother Kim? Why isn't my mother here, why are Aunt Kim and big brother Kim here?" She had a lost feeling, hoping to see her mother. She prayed, "Please do not say Mother Kim has passed away."

With mixed emotions, May hugged Aunt Kim and her big brother. She had not seen him for forty-five years. It seemed strange. "Do I know that person? He is my big brother, and she is my Aunt Kim." In her mind, she realized they were her family. Giving hugs while exchanging feelings, Aunt Kim picked up May's luggage. Aunt Kim was quiet; her brother was happy to see May, trying to talk and talk, yet May was quiet. She was too scared to ask where her mother was.

May remembered Aunt Kim as a comprehensive person. When May last saw her, she was a young lady and they talked about her boyfriends.

Aunt Kim heard May talking about boys; May said, "I could not go out with friends, I had to come home on time; if not, Mom would call my friends to ask where I was and where I was going. Overseas, you have to tell your parents where you are going and who you are with; overseas, parents are vary strict."

After that experience with Aunt Kim, May knew not to bother. At the same time, May was missing her mother. Even as a mature adult, Aunt Kim saw May as a child, a child that she had taken care of. May was defenseless; she did not want to feel that way.

May followed quietly; Aunt Kim stopped at a little restaurant, asking May, "Would you like to have something to eat? This place makes the best homemade noodles; I thought you might like to have some homemade noodles."

May thought, *I thought she might forget what l liked and what I wanted; I cannot believe she remembered.* She said out loud, "Yes, please, I would like to have some homemade noodles, I have missed them for a long time."

Aunt Kim ordered and watched as May finished her noodles. Aunt Kim and May's brother did not eat, they just sat and watched May. The noodles were as good as they were back then.

Aunt Kim explained why May's mother had not met her at the airport, saying with a choking voice, "Your mother is sick, that is why she could not make it here."

May started to cry; she was choking as the tears came down her cheeks. Her brother tried to help wipe her cheeks like May was a little girl. May pushed him away and asked Aunt Kim, "What is making her sick?"

Aunt Kim took a deep breath and said, "When she could not find you, your mom and I looked for almost two years, we put ads in newspaper for two years all over the city. We thought you died somewhere, we did not know what happened to you."

May could not help but cry. And she asked again, "How she is doing? Does she know I am here or not?" May felt guilty and said, "I am sorry and I cannot forgive myself for what I have done to my mother."

Aunt Kim explained again about May's mother; she said, "About fifteen years ago, Lee passed away, and then a fire destroyed her house and she lost everything she had. Knowing your mom, she had businesses going again and had twenty employees working for her at a restaurant, but it was too much and she had stroke and now she cannot walk."

May was choking and hurt, after all these years; she said, "She needed me, I am so sorry I was not here to help."

Aunt Kim tried to calm May and told her, "Right now you must come with me, stay with me until we know what to do with you. Your brother and I think you should stay with us."

When May heard that, she said, "I did not come here to stay permanently; what are you trying to tell me?"

Then her brother looked at May and said, "We do not want to you to go back; we don't want to lose you again."

May did not understand what Aunt Kim and her brother wanted. May began to panic; she might not go back home. May loved her two children more than anything in the world. May tried to go along with what Aunt Kim and her brother said. What they did not understand was that May was a grown woman, and she would like to be independent. But Aunt Kim and her brother did not see her as a grown woman. They saw her as the young child they remembered. They did not want May to grow up.

May was uncomfortable; Aunt Kim was cooking all her meals and cleaning the house and washing May's clothes. May tried to help in the kitchen, but Aunt Kim said, "You do not need to do that; go take a bath. When you are done, dinner should be ready."

May thought, *I must tell her I am a grown woman.* May tried, but Aunt Kim said to May, "You want to help? Okay, try to cook this fish. I would like to see how you cook it."

May was losing her nerve. She told Aunt Kim, "I do not know how to cook this fish."

Aunt Kim heard and was sharp spoken, just as May remembered. "When you left this country, you were young and had no time to learn from your mom and me, and now I see you are grown and would like to be independent, which is a good thing."

May realized Aunt Kim was testing her to see if she was grown up. But her brother said to May, "I want you to stay with us, if your children need money, we can give them whatever they need. Please stay with us; I love you, I miss you, please, I will do anything, please stay."

May was scared and uncertain. May was afraid they would lock her in all girls jail again. Shortly Aunt Kim said, "You've only been here three days and you are homesick for your children. I do not think you should stay here, you need to go back home and raise your children; they are missing you and you are missing them."

May said, "Thank you, Aunt Kim. I love you for letting me go, and I do miss my children."

The next day, May went to her mother's house, but Kim did not recognize her daughter. Mother Kim was frail, debilitated, and weak; May's stepsister hugged her, they were both crying, they had not seen each other for many years.

Mother Kim asked May with a weak voice, "Where have you been, dear? Do you understand how much I missed you?" She asked May, "Are you planning to stay this time? You must; all the family misses you, and they would love for you to stay. Please stay; how are my grandchildren doing?" Kim paused for a second and asked, "Are you getting along with your in-laws?"

When May heard "in-laws," she could not answer right away. May had to think fast and try to make an excuse about Joe's family.

May's brother saw her hesitate to answer, and he said again, "Mother was trying to tell you, you do not have to go back, if your children need money, we can send it to them. I am asking you again, please stay."

Her brother was not going to give up asking May to stay. At the same time, Kim sat quietly and looked at May; she said, "You have grown, you have been independent and Europeanized; how has your husband been treating you?"

A mother knows, a mother can feel when something is wrong. Mother Kim saw in May's face that there was some kind of problem, yet she tried to comfort her daughter. At the same time, Kim's speech was sluggish, and her face was sloping unevenly; her stroke had taken away her ability to walk, and it was strenuous to sit upright. She tried to tell May how her stepfather had passed away.

Kim was happy to see her daughter, but when she saw May's facial expression, she asked, "I see you do not look happy; how are your children doing?"

May had to answer right away. She did not want to give her mother stress; she wanted her to believe that her American husband was as good as any other man. Kim try to accept what May said, but a mother knows; Kim had been married two times and had many businesses of her own; she was still thinking sharp.

Mother Kim cried and said to May, "You do know you are those children's hope and you lead them to where they are going in the future?"

May could not help but cry, and she had to tell her mother, "I love you and I have been missing you as well as your grandson and granddaughter, but I do not know how to sort out the difficulties that family has."

Mother Kim heard and realized that May needed help. Kim explained, "Every family has some problems, but you are the solution. You brought those children into this harsh world, and you must show them who you are and lead them to where they want to go. You must be a heroine; you are there for what they need. They should be first, whatever they need. Being a mother is not easy, a mother's job is harder than any other job, yet in the end, you will enjoy it when your children are grown, knowing you have helped them get where they are." Mother Kim stopped a second, and with tears on her cheeks, she held May's hands and said, "I love you, I have missed you, I have been wondering many nights, but look at you! You have grown and you are doing fine. You must go back and help those children grow in the right direction. If not, you will regret it as a disappointment to life; you might not be happy at this moment, but you will be in the future."

May heard her mother's wise thoughts. And years of regretting undesirable sorrow began to dissolve. May could see where she was going in the future and her mother was helping. She was perplexed and had thought she was going to stay overseas for three months, but she was missing her children more and more. She spent one week with Aunt Kim and her brother and another week at Mother Kim's house. May was a grown woman, but her family could not see it. May had to stay indoors most of the time. Mother Kim was trying to help by washing her clothes, and Aunt Kim cooked meals day and night. They were overpampering her.

Mother Kim was disabled; she could not walk and talking was difficult, but she was trying to show what a good mother would do. It was too much pampering, and May said, "Mom, I am a grown woman and you do not need to pay attention to me. I can do many things myself; please stop overpampering me."

May's family was pleased to see her and loved her; at the same time, May was not as happy as she wanted to be. Her mind was on her children, and she wondered how they were doing. She was homesick. It was painstaking that she had to go home to her children. Two weeks was longer than one year.

A cousin who owned a hotel called May; she wanted her to come visit. May did not care what her cousin had or what she did. It was the same cousin who had raped her when she was young.

May had no time to confront him; May wanted to say to him, "Why did you rape me?" But she thought, there is no time to go back and relive the past. If it had not happened with her cousin, it could have been some other thing in her life; Otto and Kay might not have been in May's journey. It was time to forgive and forget; she had the courage to vindicate what happened and go home to the children she loved; it was awe-inspiring how much she loved her children.

She briefly talked with her other cousin, who explained that all the uncles had died, and her husband also passed away two years ago from natural causes. It was hurtful to hear. Again, she had to leave Korea. No running this time. She said good-bye to her mother, good-bye to her brother, good-bye to Aunt Kim, and good-bye to her stepsister. May saw who they were, and they saw who she was; she was proud to be Korean.

To her children, she was the best mother she could be, she learned how to be a mother from Kim. May was glad that her visit was good. Her mother gave her one last lecture, scolding her, yet May was glad that her mother advised her again. The following year, her stepsister called May to say her mother had passed away from a heart attack. May had unaccountable sorrow and tears of guilt for many years.

CHAPTER 23
Broken Promise, Hope to Believe

Failure is the opportunity to begin again more intelligently. You might think you know your family, but that is not real life. A promise is never to be promising, yet you must be there striving. Life is a journey, and the voyage home takes you homeward bound. May had all those thoughts. Home was a pleasant place from which to draw happiness. May had not given up hoping and believing. If you would like to have sweet fruit, you must climb the tree. As you climb, you'll have lumps, but when you reach that sweet fruit, you will smile and be glad that you climbed. If you speak honestly, then everyone will listen, and your character development is the true aim of education. To get respect from others, one must give respect to them. May was respected by many people, and she did not step on anyone on the way to the top. Time is not measured by a moment; time heals all wounds; if you have hope and believe, you will have fanciful joy. May dreamed of a journey where she could learn to become who she became.

Life is preciously preserved.

Same time surrounding harsh environment,

Pressurized by wicked evil spirit,

Whirlwind whirligig pick and swiftly zipping,

Poisoning and intoxicating to innocence,

Long period of neglect,

Tear drops became ice cold,

Let the dust off the shoulder,

Remember the good time I had,

Cool down ice-cold tears redeem with green tea,

Zest green tea becomes my life, Nothing is matter of fact.

CHAPTER 24
Trying Harder

Once you graduate from school, you may automatically enroll in the school of hard knocks. Mothers and fathers try to teach their children what is best for them. Once they leave their parents' protection, they fly free and try to stand on their own two feet, as the waves break on the shore. They may succumb to temptation and self-indulgence, asking themselves, "What is right? How do I define right? Why not left?"

If at first you don't succeed, then try harder. May's curiosity may lead to success in future. She tried to look at everything as though she were seeing it for the first time, but she hoped it was the last time filled with glory; she hoped that a good life was an agreement with nature. She used positive thinking with simplicity and clarity, and she always smiled, and her smile would make her happier day after day; she might cry last night, but she would wake up with a smile on her face and look for a brighter day to come.

May has seen the truth as she sees it; she believed her thought may change the world; she said, "I cannot change the direction of the wind, but I can adjust my sails to reach my destination." May did try hard, and instead of going to bed at night with tears on her cheeks, she would get up in the morning with a smile, with happy days to come, achieving a great goal with a smile and believe in achievement day by day.

CHAPTER 25
Hateful E-mails

E-mails often say a lot about the person who sent them. And they may hide a sneer or a cold shoulder, but they show what they are thinking. Nasty e-mails are not sent by smart and good people. They tell your son, brother, or family that the sender denigrates the person they are sent to, they are full of profanity and they dishonor and debase the person who receives them. Toby sent e-mails that aroused intense hatred. Joe and May moved away from Toby to the other side of town, but he still sent these e-mails to them. Receiving hateful e-mails was degrading but they reduced Toby's credibility; no one believed he was the father he claimed to be.

Joe and May began to receive intruding e-mails from Toby; they were intimate and full of hatred. It was irritating, and they could not stop them. They took away their pride and interfered with them. Toby was hiding in the closet, peeking out, too scared to come out of the closet, and sent hideous e-mails.

In 2010, many minorities voted in the election: Asians, Mexicans, and others. May voted with the future of her children in mind, and she was ready to support her candidate. May did not know the election would contain a conspiracy. Voters in May's city were almost 90 percent Republican. There were not many black people living there. Only forty years ago, there were only one or two Asians living there, where May lived in the same place and same house, raising her children, where May called home sweet home. May thought the election was a time to help people of all colors form a community with color-blind people. May had no experience in voting, yet she had the courage to go to City Hall, give her name, and line up with others giving their opinion. May did it herself, and it felt good to vote in 2010.

She came home and tried to relieve the tension; there was an e-mail, which always led to an emotional outburst. The family knew May voted for change, and they began to send May harassing e-mails. May cannot forget some of the comments in these e-mails, like saying the first lady was dancing with the president, and they said "the way she was dancing, it was like she was mopping the floor!"

May was shocked at what the person said; she responded, "You cannot say that! It does not matter who she is or what she was wearing, she is the first lady; when I saw her dancing with the president, it was beautiful! Please do not say it again!" May stopped a second and added, "You guys are reading too much on the Internet!"

She thought she knew that person. Sometimes, the true person comes out. Others received the same e-mail, and she knew it was from Dan, Joe's big brother.

"Is this really from my big brother?" Joe asked many times.

Dan's e-mail began with, "Alas, where has all our innocence gone?"

After the burial service at Sue's graveside, a massive clap of thunder was followed by a tremendous bolt of lightning, and then even more cacophonous thunder; they looked at the pastor and calmly said, "Well, she's there. The end may be happiness in your world and in your heart."

Joe read the e-mail, and he soon went into a stage of anger and said to May, "I am so sorry for this junk e-mail that my big brother sent; he is a cold-hearted person; we just buried our mother." That e-mail was an insult to May. Joe took a deep breath, but he needed it to blow out. He ran out the door and screamed, "F#%&, go to hell!"

May could see what he saw. Dan was jealous of May and Joe. After Sue was buried, Joe and May went to visit the grave many times. They brought many wreaths and flowers to show how much they cared for and missed their mother. Yet Dan and Lake did not visit their mother's grave once. Toby visited once and saw all the flowers on the gravestone.

One day, Dan visited the grave yard after going to the doctor's office; he saw all that Joe and May had done. It was eye-opening, and he was stupefied. Toby could not help bragging about Joe and May to Dan; he said, "Look at this, all the flowers have her name written with the date, with love; look at how the colors highlight the grave stone, I was going to come here and put some grass on top of her, but I do not have to, my goodness they have done a good job!"

Toby began to weep and weep. Dan could not take his bragging about Joe and May, and he asked Toby to go home. After that, Dan sent them an e-mail that said, "I was visiting Mom's grave, it was nice what you guys have done to her headstone."

May believed that they could trust Dan and talk to him when they had a problem. After that e-mail, she thought, "Should I trust him or not?" May knew that Toby had been intimidating, harassing, and discriminating against people of every color. To Dan, this was an unexpected bombshell; May refused to believe Dan was a narrow-minded person, but the e-mail tells all. From one day to the next, he would be a nice brother and ask Joe to forgive him; he sent an e-mail saying, "Happy big brother day."

Dan's e-mail also said, "Love all the people and treat them right. Forgive me once. Get a second chance. If you do, grab it with both hands. If it changes your life, let it. Take a few minutes to think before. Forgive quickly."

May had forgiven and forgiven. She liked to talk face to face and eye to eye, saying, "Sorry, let us start all over again." May had not heard from both sides, but someone's e-mail said to Joe, if not Toby, "I would like to forgive and start all over again with Joe and May."

"But have you heard from Lake and Dan?"

There was no phone call, but another e-mail agitated them and provoked egotism. May looked for an example that both sides agreed that what had happened was yesterday and today would begin anew.

Dan sent another discriminating e-mail to Joe and May, saying, "We thought you might like this." The e-mail began with, "Stamp malfunction." Stamps were not sticking to envelopes. Presidential commissioner presented the following findings: #1, the stamps were in perfect order, #2, there was nothing wrong with the glue, #3, people were licking the wrong side. Dan called himself a big brother and had three boys; was this how he taught young men? Did Dan know May and Joe?

Dan sent that e-mail, which allowed May and Joe to look at big brother; they thought they knew him but he completely destroyed their trust and respect. Joe and May understood that Dan had served this country as a responsible person. That e-mail showed he was like his father, living faithlessly and seeing racist jokes against people of color. Again, Dan could not see this as racist. He was not going to stop, and he continued to send unfair e-mails again and again; he said, "This e-mail came from my friend JJ; I told him, this is not politically correct, and please do not ever send me politically incorrect racist stuff again, then I laughed pretty bad, it is funny and you might like it too. I can't stop laughing."

The e-mail was about Muslims: "Muslim culture meets German, Muslim engineering sold German cars! This is an actual German TV commercial. Can you image this on American TV? Ha, ha, ha."

May's point was not about Muslim culture, it was about whether you agree or not; if you think it is not correct, then erase the e-mail. Dan was laughing at that joke and then sent it to Joe, saying, "It is funny! Ha, ha, ha."

While Dan was laughing with his friends, he did not say it was not politically correct and racist. He was hiding in the closet, laughing with Toby and Lake as well as his friends. He could not come out of the closet.

One day May asked Dan, "Where are all these e-mails coming from?"

Dan answered, "I do not know, my wife June has been sending them to our friends!"

It was funny, because most of the e-mails were in Dan's name. If the e-mails came from June, they said nothing about her in them.

They knew Dan was lying. You never know behind the person, even though you think you know. Dan was hiding behind these e-mails; they could not help that their trust was gone.

Toby also sent e-mails that were hateful. These e-mails went to all the grandchildren, to the family, and to his friends. The e-mails were filled with hate.

May and Joe knew that when they got an e-mail from Toby, then it would not be good; they would not open the e-mail, saying, "There is no reason to open this e-mail."

What Toby did not know was that none of his seven grandchildren believed in hating like he did. Otto knew not to discriminate against other races and colors. Otto was taught to behave with integrity, and he was never allowed to hit women, or to steal, or lie; he learned to always tell the truth. As Otto grew up, he learned to live with integrity.

Toby did not see how Otto was educated by May, so he sent these e-mails to Otto, thinking his grandson would agree with him. But Toby was wrong. The e-mails were out of touch, like the one Dan sent to Joe about Muslims selling cars to Germans.

Otto could not take these e-mails; they were full of hate, and they discriminated against people of all colors. Otto sent Toby an e-mail saying, "The e-mails I have been receiving are not funny; please do not send me any more politically incorrect e-mails."

Toby responded, "I had no idea you thought that way, and you have spoken."

After that, Otto did not receive any more e-mails from Toby. That was okay, because he did not have to hear Toby's language of hate.

One day Joe got a phone call from Dan; he had gotten an e-mail from Lake, saying that Toby had baked a cake for her and Junk. Dan said to Joe, "I do not remember our dad ever cooking when we were home, did he?"

Joe thought back and said, "No, he did not ever cook once, Mom was always in the kitchen cooking and canning."

Dan was confused, thinking about Toby's unusual behavior; Lake also sent Dan a picture of her with Toby. Dan was wondering that what was about; he asked Joe, "What is going on in that house?" Toby was baking cakes for their sister and cooking her meals. What was he was saying?

Lake sent Dan a picture from Veterans Day. It was the first year Toby attended the ceremony at City Hall without Sue. Lake was hugging Toby. Her e-mail said, "Here I am with my dad." She should have said "with *our* dad."

Lake was making the point that he was *her* dad. When Dan received that e-mail, he called Joe to explain all the details and ask what was going on there with Toby. May could not answer, but she did know that Lake had not stopped by Sue's grave yard, not once. She was living in the house, and their mother was no longer living the house.

With that, Joe said to May, "My sister, that B@#$, is taking over our mother's place; she kicked Mother to the curb; my father cannot control that B@#$. I wondered why all these years. That nice Junk can go to hell!" Joe stopped a second and screamed, "I always said to myself, Junk could be my @#$ brother, guess who has taken out our e-mail? B@#$ sister has our father all to herself."

May did not care about the e-mails from Toby. Joe made a statement that was too strong. Lake's life was nothing but a lie; she "lied her way to get out of danger; a cock-and-bull story would get her out of a situation; lying was her problem."

May thought that all those e-mails were trash; she tried not to think about what Joe said, the e-mails were nothing but harassment, a preconceived opinion with a premeditated person who was like a worm living in the ground. At this moment, the relationship between Toby and Lake did not matter, as long as she did not hear from him or receive intimate, harassing, or discriminating e-mails. It began with e-mails and ended with e-mails. For now, it was no longer important, it no longer mattered: father to son or to grandson or daughter, the trust was broken with trash e-mail.

CHAPTER 26
All Aspects

For many reasons, we live in the face of double standards, the limitations to our lives is only in our minds, yet if we can use our imagination, then the possibilities are limitless, but how good is our imagination? Now we live with revised and modified revolution in fundamental government; the same person is our teacher, doctor, lawyer, and many others. Others are living in an imagination that raising a family is the most important thing. May learned from her ancestors and her mother; she tried to do the best she could. Sometimes, she repressed her feelings.

Many of us look and think that someone will comment on what we do; if not, we point to the person and say, "So nice, she smiles all the time." May asked, "With that smile, what does that person want with her smile?"

May's view was, "The smile is often misleading with someone who is two-faced." It brings treachery and dishonesty, with people scheming to be crafty. It is part of a game a person plays to keep from getting caught, or trying to be nice to get some information. With that information, they will mock her and laugh it off. How nice was that person? You thought a nice person is always good?

May was working in an accounting office as an AP clerk; it was good-paying job, and had a hundred-plus employees. That time she was young and had no experience. Luckily, she went to a local college and studied accounting, which helped her get the job. Unfortunately, there were rumors about how she got that job; she is Asian so she had to be as good as an angel. Her language was given to miscommunication. Figures of speech were often misunderstood. At that time, Joe had lost his job and stayed home with the children. May was stressed that she could not be there with the children; a mother should be cooking dinner. She needed help but Joe did not. Going to classes and going to work with no help was not easy. Yet May wanted to work and stay in school. When she went to work, even with all the pressure, May had a smile on her face.

She told her coworkers, "I am smiling to you, please accept my smile and be my friends." She did not say that she thought if she was nice, then they might be nice back. Most of the time, that does work, but there is always one who has some evilness, they are so nice to you but later you find that the nice person was your enemy. In May's case, it was Carol, who was so nice and comforting; May thought she could talk to Carol anything, but it was not true.

One day, her supervisor called May and asked, "What happened to the data sheet?"

May asked, "I do not understand; what happened to the data sheet?"

The boss said, "The number are not correct."

May thought she should not question her supervisor, so she said, "I do not know what happened, I will be more careful next time. I am sorry."

The supervisor did not accept May's politeness, and she did not want to stop arguing; she said, "I understand you have a problem with your husband and he is not working right now."

May asked, "Who told you? How do you know about my husband losing his job?"

The boss was glad to get May's attention and said, "It was Carol, your friend and coworker."

May could not believe it; the only person she told was Carol. Yet May should have learned some lessons from overseas. May did not learn from her mistakes. May thought Carol would be like the friends she had in childhood, but it brought back the betrayal by a friend.

Later, she found the mistake on the data sheet was not May's fault, it was a computer programmer who had misplaced a number. Whether that was done with Carol's intention, May cannot say, but it broke up a good relationship.

Every country has good, bad, and ugly with happy relationship. It is human nature to see where someone else is falling. They do not look at themselves as the downfall of others. There are many nice people, and friends and many others.

June was known as nice, and she could bake sweets. She could cook with sugar, cookies, cakes, and anything with chocolate. Every family gathering, she made something with sugar, known as "Aunt June's sweet." She was sweet and could cook sweets. And she acted nice to May as well as to Joe. But was the niceness real? If it was real, then she should not have told May what she said about flat faces and short legs.

May heard the comments from June. June was only talking about what she saw on TV. With that attitude, who has not had a bad day, and how much can we do to make a bad day into a good day? Many of us have bad days and good days.

One summer, May did not take summer vacation; she took a writing class. It was a hot summer; May thought this class could be her hope and future. She said, "If I finish this classes, then I only have to take another year to finish up and earn my degree." May was looking forward to finishing college.

Earlier that morning, she was dragging her book bag, trying to rush and weave among the students. Then someone pushed in front of May, brushing with her arm, rushing into the gate. May thought, *Okay, and slow down. No reason to rush, we have time for almost other fifteen minutes.* She did not take offense, but she was quiet. She told herself, *No reason to be angry at that person because she brushed with her arm, she has bad attitude, and ignore that person, do not let that bother me.*

May knew after many years in this country, there are all kinds of people, both good and bad. She learned to smile if she can, learned to ignore it if she had to. In her class, everyone else was young and American. Out of twenty-five students, only three were Asian; May was there to learn how to write, which would help in her next classes. She was eager to finish and looked for a future job that could help her climb the corporate ladder.

All the students were glad and wanted to succeed, they were cheerful, and they got to know their classmates. They interacted reciprocally with each other. In twenty minutes, the teacher walked into the classroom. In a second, all the students got quiet, they looked at the teacher, who was a big woman, and May knew the person in the front was the teacher. Overseas, a teacher is a hero to the students, the students can learn from that person and look up to them

May added, "The teaching job is not easy, the teaching job has to be equal attention to every students, no matter what color, what age, be a role model to the community as well as to the school and to your country."

May tried to get along with the teacher; overseas, when she went to school, May was always a good student; she had a good relationship with her teachers, back in high school. Most Asian students have problems with the language; there is a lack of communication in English. For adults, learning a second language is more complex. May was mighty good at math, but she had problems with English. She tried and tried, but it was hard. May always asked her teachers every time she could not understand something, and this teacher was bothered and annoyed by May's frequent questioning. The teacher was not going to help May.

The teacher was always mocking May and looking to get even with her. May wondered what she was trying to show her. After two weeks, there was an essay test, and May did not understand how many points the teacher was going to give students for the test.

May wondered how many points the test would be worth, and she raised her hand and asked, "How many points are we getting for this?"

The teacher did not say how many points, and all the students agreed with May; a few students asked the teacher at the same time, "Yes, teacher, how many points are we getting from this?"

You could see the teacher's face getting red, and she said in front of all the other students, "I hate teaching ESL students!"

The other students in class looked at May, they were at a loss of what to say; their eyes were opened to the teacher, who had acted repulsively.

Sometimes someone lives in your neighborhood who is always snooping like a goose, looking for a weakling person. May was not a weak person to be picked on by a peeping Tom. May lived in the same house for almost thirty-five years; many neighbors moved in and out. And on holidays, they had to be the first ones to decorate their yards with ornaments: Christmas, Thanksgiving, Halloween. People would sneak around and gossip about who had the best decorations in their yard.

On Halloween, the children came around asking for candy. In the hot summer, families were outside for barbecues, the aroma of beef and chicken made people hungry for the dinner table. One house had a deceptive, lying person; he was a peeping Tom. This neighbor moved from the deep south and impersonated a top pop star. He looked and acted like that pop star. This neighbor did not use the N word; he did not act like a redneck.

Every summer, May and Joe worked on their yard, on the trees, on their summer garden, and on their lawn. This peeping Tom and his wife always mocked May and Joe. They would bring their dog outside their yard and let him bark. The husband would yell at his wife and call her a bitch; Joe heard the peeping Tom yell names at his wife, he knew he was outside the fence watching what May and Joe were doing. They did not want attention from the peeping Tom, yet he was there, next to their house.

"What we can do to the ignore these people? Just ignore!"

Big men and women like to pick on the weakest link. They are malevolent, devious, and evasive. Nevertheless, in any event, Toby acted like a big man with a big ego, if not proud, then envious and jealous. Toby would always comment whenever he saw a woman, he would gush and be overbearing in his sexual attention.

Toby's famous phrase was, "Sit on my lap, let me help you to relax."

Toby would touch women and rub their neck with his big farmer's hands. He thought he was cunning, and when he was rubbing a woman's neck, he would do that to himself and slobber all over her. Most women would know that he was fondling her.

If he could not share his sexual needs with any other woman in the family, then he would not say anything good about them. May would not give him sexual attention, so he treated her like a second class person. Toby tried to compete with little woman May, showing he was the man and overwhelm her.

May said, "I cannot call him a big man, he is not desirable, he is vulgar and gives me the creeps up my spine." May had to ask Joe, "How do you see your father?"

Joe's answer was simple as can be: "I did not know back then, I thought it should been that way, now I have learned from you and many others over the years that what I saw is not acceptable and he is not a good father. I am deeply hurt."

Joe became like Toby with putting women down and thinking they were weak; he had jealousy and resentment.

May answered what Toby said: "That is not true, I think she is beautiful and she can be; why not?"

Many women had a good education and did good, but some are good looking and are not there to help, no matter what they do. Looking around, even if you have been educated for sixteen years, you may be living without a home and helping your forty-year-old son who has no job skills, trying to helping him stay out of jail. May paid for her own education. Lake's children, Junk and Cary, went to college on a government grant. Are they successful?

They are not, and where did all the money go? How much of that money was taken from the government in a scam? How many take advantage of and manipulate and abuse the system? Otto learned from Toby and wanted to be like him. He saw how Toby talked to and treated women. Otto began to drink and do drugs, making him exaggerate. After a few years of alcohol poisoning, Otto began to act like his grandfather. Otto's modest, innocent ego was no longer excited. He would lash out at women, saying, "Look at that woman driver."

May did not like what she heard; she said to Otto, "What did you say? I live this city with pride; don't complain about how she drives. You do not know her, and you cannot talk like that; you do not know that person! You went to school here; what is the matter with you? Have you forgotten? I told you do not ever hurt a woman."

Otto regretfully acknowledged that he was offensive. May did not argue, she knew that he did not care about Toby. May could not tell Otto his grandfather was no good. Toby was worthless, but he thought he was a patriot. Toby and Otto did not know there are many women who were heroes in this country. These women were admired for their nobility, courage, and outstanding achievements.

Heroes are quiet, fair, and care about others. They do not call names, intimidate, or bully. After all, the bully is a loser with no dreams.

Joe worked on himself to May. Joe's poor eating habits came from Toby and were passed to Otto. Joe ate sweet and high-fat foods. Joe's feeding habits affected May and put an end to May's beliefs. Joe tried to follow Toby's footsteps, putting down women with the attitude of a raised eyebrow. Joe sat back and watched; he let May do the hard work with the children. May navigated without a navigator, she become a bad person, and pushed and criticized the children.

May realized that she had time to let go of her own dreams. Joe was two different people, he sat back with easy money and short cut hand-me-downs. Among obstacles, Lake had more than anyone in the family with a particular direction given by family, government grants, and jobs, and more and more; she liked to take the easy money. But Lake did not just go there to catch. Rather, she was living with falsehoods. She was in and out of relationships that yielded to a downfall. Joe tried to poison May's mind. But May believed and dreamed that education was the top of everything. May was not going to go down as a coward. May fought back with the last drop of strength; she stood firmly on her own two feet. May's beliefs were stronger than her speech.

CHAPTER 27
Flip-flops

Today is the tomorrow that we worried about yesterday. As we go along, some stay on their feet and others follow along, looking for the footprints. One day, Toby wanted to drive, the next day he decided he wanted to go with them, flip-flopping in and out.

Dan asked Toby, "Would you like to go live with other retired people? The soldier's home might be a good place to live; you might enjoy it."

All visiting the soldier's home, Toby decided he wanted to go live there. After six months, he changed his mind; he no longer wanted to live in the soldier's home, but Dan had already made a down payment on a nearby condominium.

Six months later, Toby changed his mind again and said, "I decided I *would* like to stay here."

Dan lost his down payment on the condominium. After that, he did not trust in the father-and-son relationship. Dan came less often to visit Toby; sometimes, he went three to six weeks without hearing from Dan, and Toby cried to Joe, asking why Dan did not call and stop by. One day May and Joe stopped by with Toby's favorite foods: soup and homemade noodles. Toby was crying that he did not want to go to the soldier's home and did not know what he wanted to do.

May asked Toby, "What do you want? You like to stay here or go there? What make you happy?"

When Toby heard "what makes you happy," his eyes lit up and he said, "I love it here, this place was where your mom and I were happy."

Joe and May said to Toby, "Then stay; if it makes you happy, then you should stay here."

After dinner, May asked Toby, "How can this place benefit you?"

It was wrong for May to ask, and he was defensive and said with anger, "I might change my mind tomorrow!"

May did not argue with Toby; she did not say anything, learning from mistakes long ago to say nothing, rather that what was on her mind. When your child or husband is two faced, they hurt you. Trying to make the best out of what you have, then your husband may be wrong and take all your energy.

One day Otto said to May, in front of his girlfriend, "I am thinking of converting to Catholicism."

May thought to herself, "What did he say? What?" May was screaming inside her mind, she could not believe his statement; she said, "I think he is out of his mind."

Otto grew his hair long and rode a loud, noisy bike. He looked like a thug, like a menacing bully; he was proud to be a biker.

"What happened to him wanting to be a Catholic? Whatever he wants to be is okay, he wants to be a Catholic or be a biker, but he should not bully others, he should not call his mother names."

May could not say anything and look at Otto, flip-flopping in and out. One day he was motivated to save the earth. Otto did not care that he himself was smoking and drinking more than he should be, hanging out with his friends. Yet, he was like Toby and Joe, flip-flopping and arguing.

Joe only paid attention to his own life, he was raw and ruthless, he had hidden his two-faced flip-flopping with anger in and out from life; he said to May, "I love you."

May said to him, "What does this have to do with love? One day you scream and the next day everything is going to be good, I do not understand."

When he was talking to family, laughing and carrying on himself, May thought he was missing home with friends and family.

Joe was cold-hearted as ever and said to May, "I am so sorry that you could not go see your family and talk to them."

May's feeling was, "Joe wants me to be in his world, lost in the woods. Joe was fed up with negative, arrogant, and bad influences that impel May's mind and emotions. I have fought back with positive thoughts and emotions, and I know that I can do it." May paused a few minutes and took a deep breath; she said, "Many times I thought I would give up; he was using my emotions to get there. All that hurt by him is more than I could name; I feel he used me emotionally, mentally, and most of all with my pride. Joe played the game and took away from me many things I cannot name, but I am going to let it go; I have no love for him or his family."

CHAPTER 28
Realism Loss of Soul

"We looked around his garden and he found an empty place. We then looked down upon this earth and saw your tired face. We put arms around you and lifted you to rest. Our garden must be beautiful, and he always takes the best. We knew you were in pain. We knew that you would never get well on earth again. We saw the road was getting rough and the hills were hard to climb, so he closed your weary eyelids and whispered, 'Peace be to thine.' It broke our hearts we were losing you, but you did not go alone, for part of us went with you the day he called your home."

As Joe answered the phone call, he drew breath in convulsive gasps with weeping, he could not stop sobbing. The sorrow and pain were real. Joe did not think Sue was going to go that early. It was hurtful and sad, May thought back to her mother, Kim, it doubled the sadness and she could not stop sobbing. In some sense, May knew Sue was leaving sometime soon. Sue gave May a beautiful beaming angel smile three days before she died. And Sue waved good-bye to May before leaving this world. Sue was preparing herself on the day of May and Joe's visit. Sue let May and Joe know that she was going away. Certainly, the phone call confirmed that Sue had passed away.

May and the children, Otto and Kay, wished to go pay their

last respects to Sue. Kay had not seen Toby in a long time and wondered how to face him, but life moved on whether one acts like a coward or hero, one must face the truth with respect. May helped Otto and Kay decide what clothes to wear, but she did not say anything about her loss and disappointment; she was sad that her two mothers were gone. May was missing her mother unspeakably.

At the service, Otto sat in the front with the other grandchildren, who were pallbearers. In the town where Toby and Sue had been married, there were many people who remembered Sue. The friends and family gathered in the chapel. Before she sat down, May kissed Sue's forehead. Sue was cold and stiff, which made May spin; for a second, she lost her balance, but she managed to stand firm and lead the children to the front seat. People were sitting quietly in respect, but at the last minute, Junk walked in and came to the front row, asking where he should sit. Lake showed her son Junk where to sit, and he sat in a chair on the end.

Dan's last child was not there to pay his respects. This was easy to understand; he was married twice, and the first time when he married, rebelling against Toby, he took his wife's last name and gave up the family name. When he did this, Toby wrote him a disagreeable letter, disowning him. It was quarrelsome, disgusting, and repulsive. The day of the funeral, a family function, Sue was not respected.

May thought, "That was a problem then, now is the time for him to show respect to his grandmother. I was young and did not know that I could have kept our family name, but I loved my grandmother and respected her."

In time, the chaplain spoke and said how sorry he was that this grandmother and mother and wife had died, but she was in heaven with loving care. And she loved everyone in her family.

But the chaplain did not mention Toby's name; instead, he said, "Miss Sue is gone, her husband is here, and if anyone wants to speak about Sue, then this is the time to say so, please raise your hand!"

The seating had been devised into two sections. The people on the right hand side were from Toby and Sue's family. There were mostly second and third cousins, and the people on the left were mainly friends from high school who had grown up with Sue and Toby. Many people from the family spoke about how nice she was and she was going to be missed, but no one mentioned Toby.

One person sitting among the friends raised his hand on the air; the chaplain pointed to him, and he began to speak; he said, "I went to school with Sue, she was the nicest person you could meet, but the man she married, Toby, was the most obnoxious person I have ever known, he was a revolting, disgusting, and abhorrent person; therefore, Sue is better off in heaven, and we are going to miss her a lot."

The man sat remorsefully as he released the years of hate in his mind that he had wanted to say to Toby. The chapel was soundless as can be; no one stood to defend Toby. The man sat quietly. May looked at Toby to see his reaction; his face was crinkled on the edges of his mouth, he was rubbing his face with a stiff hand, and he was looking at the floor, not saying one word.

At that moment, the chaplain knew he needed to be moving on; he had no reason to defend Toby, and he praised Sue, saying, "She is going to receive loving care and peace in heaven."

Afterward, everyone came together in the chapel cafeteria for coffee and sandwiches; May was thinking she should give Lake her condolences; what had happened was over, now was the time to make peace and look for the future with no envy, no mocking, and helping each other. There were almost fifty people in that room, and more people were outside.

Otto was visiting with the cousins. Shortly, Kay noticed Debbie, Lake's only granddaughter, wearing a short dress and high heels. Kay walked over and said to May, "I am going to say hi to my niece; I will also tell her she is not old enough to wear high heel shoes, and she should not wear those kind of clothes to Grandmother's funeral."

May had no time stop Kay from saying that to Debbie; it was too late. In a second, there was Debbie, all smiling and glad to see her Aunt Kay; Kay raised her eyebrow and said in a biting tone, "Hi sister! I think you are too young to wear those high heel shoes!"

Kay did not understand that this would make Debbie want to bite her in the future. Debbie ran and told Lake what Kay said to her.

In a short time, May saw Lake coming in from outside; May rushed over to Lake and said, "I am so sorry for your mother."

Lake said hastily, "What do you think, my mother just passed away!"

May thought, *Okay, you do not want to accept peace; we're not getting anywhere.*

Later, May found that Kay was trying to tell Lake that she was sorry that her mother was gone. Lake said to Kay, "What do you think, my mother just passed away!"

Even while the family was honoring their mother, Lake seemed to have problems accepting condolences for Sue. Everyone in the family was sad and hurt; they missed Sue's soft-spoken love.

But Lake kept saying, "My mother, my mother," trying to show the family she cared about their mother; Lake pointed the blame at them.

Lake accused May and Kay as being the roughnecks to others.

Kay never had the chance to visit like other grandchildren, staying overnight or spending time with Sue one-on-one, like many other things that grandparents share.

Their relationship with their grandfather was so cold; May could only say to Kay and Otto, "I am so sorry."

A month later, the favorite uncle passed away. All the cousins were there to grieve for their uncle. They served finger food and they all talked and shared good memories. At last, May saw Lake come from the other room to sit beside Joe. Joe knew not to bother Lake with any comments about their mother or father.

While visiting, one of the cousins said, "I understand cousin Vicky wrote a book."

Joe said, "I did not know Vicky wrote a book; what was it about?"

Lake acted like an immature woman and recalled what happened a month ago, when Kay criticized Lake's grandchild; Lake had not forgotten, and this was the perfect time to insult Joe. She asked Joe with a sneer, "It is on Amazon; don't you know how to read? Don't you know how look at Amazon?"

May was flabbergasted and overwhelmed at the scornful abuse; she could not bear the humiliation. May screamed silently, *You say what? I cannot read? Then how can I help with all the homework, helping Joe's problem with math, and many other issues? Do you know or even care?*

May looked at Lake and said to the family, "Lake needs to grow up as an adult, instead of staying in childhood in the lecherous relationship with her father, and her failed marriage is not something to be written about."

May knew she had been outcast to this family, and so had Joe, but they had given this family more than anyone, and this was the time to leave the family. There was no reason to fight or attack this wicked, immoral family."

One last example, it was the first Christmas Joe was without his mother. Joe cried and wanted to go to see his mother's grave. For five months, he had memories of Sue, her smile, her soft voice and gentle touch, her hugs, and many more. It seemed like yesterday she was cooking homemade noodles in the kitchen. He looked at the headstone; no one else had gone there to take care of it. Just the fresh dirt reminded him that she had been gone for months.

Joe started choking, but he tried not to show it. May looked at the person next to them, he was covering a grave in a green Christmas blanket, and one other person had left some flowers. But Sue's grave had nothing to show anyone cared, just the grass on top of her.

One day, May cooked her favorite food and soup that could be frozen and ready to eat; they brought them to Toby's house. His guest bathroom used to be filled with Sue's favorite photos. When they visited, Joe went to the bathroom, but all the photos were taken out, and many other things of his mother's were not there.

Sue had been erased within one week. Dan called Joe and said, "Lake is changing the guest bathroom and has taken out all Mom's photos and redoing it with her own things."

Joe did not know what to think; he was mad as a lost puppy looking for his mother; he could not accept she was gone forever. Then he thought about Lake crying, "My mother and my mother."

May had not seen one tear coming from Lake. "Where is Lake's love of her mother? Is she that cold? No feeling for her mother, that she is not going to come back. For that could have been just one time go see how her mother was doing."

One evening, Toby called Joe and said, "How are you doing? You are the only person to stop by and see Mom's grave; no one, not your brother or your sister, stops by your mother's grave, not even one time."

Toby was crying; he was lonely and missed his wife; he said, "You are doing a good job for your mother; I should stop by the grave more often."

Joe tried to calm down his father's emotions, yet how could he express to him how much he loved his mother? May saw that Joe was stressed by talking to Toby; she said, "A family with a black heart is too cold to comfort."

CHAPTER 29
Attach Oneself To

It was hard to spend the first St. Valentine's Day without Sue. Every young child's memory of Valentine's Day is being loved by their mother. As they grow, they find their own lover and share the day with them. Outcast by Joe's family, May had no intention of going to any family gathering. Joe missed every holiday and family gathering. The first year without Sue, Joe wanted to go out to eat, at the same time, he could not say May was with him. May and Joe wanted to have dinner at the same restaurant. After dinner, a server brought flowers to May; they were carnations, which in Asia means a long life.

May was happy as a little girl in front of Joe, showing joy and bragging, "Look, Joe, she brought me a flower." Joe showed joy and was glad May received flowers from the server. May did not see Joe's jealousy. Even May was thinking, *When we go shopping, he is going to get me a rose.* May was thinking wrong with Joe's dumfounded carelessness.

Going into a supermarket, Joe always pushed the shopping cart; sometimes he mocked her and asked for Starbucks coffee. All the cashiers knew when May came, and the server asked, "Did you get a flower from your husband?"

May answered, "Yes, we went out to eat and the server gave me a flower, it was nice."

Joe heard all that and ignored it. May was all happy, and what Joe did at that moment does not matter. Shopping for what they needed each week, they found canned goods on sale. May and Joe were near the flower shop. May thought, *Joe is going to get some flowers for me.* She was all excited and naturally high. Her husband went close to the flower shop; Joe looked in for one second, turned to the left, and ignored the flower shop. He walked away as fast as he could.

May tried to catch Joe, thinking in her mind, *I was wrong; what was I thinking? He has not bought me flowers for St. Valentine's Day in almost thirty-five years. I must move on; I have not had a lover in almost thirty-five years, I must not cry about flowers, someday I'll have a lover again.*

May walked beside Joe, feeling distant from him. A worker passed by, and Joe smiled at her with a big grin, beaming from ear to ear. May realized that Joe was not happy with her. One day they went out to eat, and a lady passing by looked at Joe; he made eye contact with a big smile.

May saw and said to Joe, "There was a connection with her, your eyes are beaming."

Joe tried to defend himself by saying, "She had too much mascara on her eyes."

May looked at Joe and said, "It is okay, you do not have to make excuses. I understand."

In many ways Joe had let May go a long time ago. That Valentine's Day after dinner, Joe wanted to call his dad.

May thought, *Okay, when did he become a nice son? Now he wants to call Dad without me telling him to call Dad and say hi.*

Joe told May in an unfriendly tone, "Turn down the TV!"

May looked at him and said, "Whatever."

Every time Joe called his dad, Toby would answer; on that night, it was Lake who answered; they just had dinner and Toby was washing the dishes. Lake began to tell Joe, "I am getting rid of Mom's stuff, you want anything?"

Joe's answer was, "I have no idea what you are trying to get rid of."

Lake tried to explain and Toby got onto the extension, as she said, "If you want anything, stop by. I'd be glad to drag everything out to the living room and show you!"

The way Lake said "drag everything out to the living room" was uncaring; her language was cold, and it intensely frustrated Joe. And then she asked, "Do want to talk to Dad?"

Joe did not want to, yet he had to and he asked Toby, "Yes I do, is it okay with you?"

May heard what he said and wondered, Why does he need his sister's permission to talk his dad?

This did not make anything clear. Toby answered with a happy voice and explained, "Well, she cooks and I wash the dishes; everything is going good, I had a doctor's checkup and should hear from the doctor next week."

Joe was glad and asked Toby, "You are doing good? I am glad to hear that." His father's answer was, "She is the mom and I am her dad."

When Joe heard what Toby said, he did not know what to say or what to think; Joe shook his head and said, "Uh, uh, uh."

May looked at Joe; he was lost and angry. It was a short call, and

Joe said good-bye to Toby and cut the call short. As he put the phone down, Joe's face was red as a beet; he screamed, "You never know what is going on that house, she is giving b#@# jobs!"

May tried to calm Joe down and asked, "What is matter with you? And what do you mean, b#@# job?" Of course, May had no idea of what a b#@# job was, and Joe said, "You are never going to find out!"

May did not know what to think but she said, "You left me on St. Valentine's Day with jealousy, you thought you'd get attention from Lake and Toby. It did not happen, instead, you were snake bit by Lake and Toby!"

Treachery and dishonesty made love betray a relationship with nutty self-assertion. Talking to Joe was nice and acceptable to anyone. He spoke softly and with an innocent smile; no one saw his mendaciousness or his tyrannical, malignant stony heart.

May could not find Joe's play: namely, moving to the city, getting a house with the children, staying in a job, and providing what the family needed; it is the parents' job.

Joe said to May, "Well, thirty-four years ago, he lost his job; at that time I was young, too young to understand what was going on around me. Without any experience, I could not get a job, the bills had to be paid, we had to pay the mortgage, we had to heat the house, and most of all, food had to go on the dinner table; where could we go to get the money to pay the bills and put food on the table? Look at my hand; do you see a wedding ring? No, we had to sell my wedding ring to pay the bills and put food on the table."

May had tears running down her cheeks; she choked with the memory. As a coward and weakling, Joe did not try to replace his wedding ring. May said, "Joe left me thirty-four years ago in many ways. I did not see and I have failed. Joe has been making me believe that he loves me with his heart, but he only loves me as some woman to show his family and friends that he got what he wanted out from me. At the same time, he might win with his mind game, but he did not win integrity with the two children. Joe failed to unify his family. As a father, he was not approachable to Otto and Kay; he might have been a nice dad, but fatherhood and being a nice father and a nice husband is no longer possible."

May redeemed herself and said, "I've become sage; I am canny and shrewd, worldly as to how good my life can be from now on. For now, Joe is my best friend; I have no feelings for him as a lover or husband. I am letting him go free. I have no regrets, no anger, no foreboding, I have made myself at peace and will be quietly restful. For now we leave as friends and business partners, and when it comes to be, then it will be."

May did not know how many years it had been since he held her hand, or had an intimate relationship with her, or said something comforting to her. May had been without a man all her life.

She would answer "What is your life experience?" with, "I cannot stand a man with a big ego, with that attitude, they pick on little women and bully them, they are mean and try to compare themselves with the wind; being greedy does not make him a man, it just shows me he is another person who is low-down, despicable, and vile, it reminds me of Toby, he might say to family he is the man, in my mind, I wish I never met him and do not care about him. It seems coldhearted, but more than anyone, he has hurt my family and I will not trust him as long as I am alive, he is not a good man, he needs help."

Toby robbed Joe's dream, his child's dream; that is not all. I saw him as a criminal; he took Sue's soul with artificial feelings; with his sexual thrills, he pretended to be innocent and told many people that he loved that child or loved that person. Without sorrow, he has no heart, he has no dreams, he is not a good man.

May added, "I have forgiven what he did to my family, because he is not a smart person, showing what's wrong or right, he just loves himself, nothing but himself, does not care, doing all the bad things to please himself, it just harms and hurts himself. He calls it love, but he does not know what love is, after all, he is my children's grandfather."

CHAPTER 30
Push to Giving It Up to Moving Out

Being a grandfather and father does not give you the right to decide where a person wants to go and stay in life. When someone's spouse is gone, it is a lonely road. Toby was just like any other person, living with lonely heart, even trying to be less offensive and demeaning, living with two sons and a daughter with seven grandchildren. May would not say he was a good man, but she would give him credit for surviving and not surrendering. Toby wanted to stay in his house to remember Sue. Good things and bad things, his last thoughts were that he would not give it up.

Less than a week after Sue died, Dan said to Toby, "Lake and I are thinking, you should move into a retirement home; that's the place you should be moving into, Dad!"

Dan was pushing and Lake was on the same page as Dan. At that time they wanted Toby to go away after Sue was gone, the next day. Toby fought to stay in that house. The following week, Lake was going into Sue's closets and collecting her clothes and wearing them, taking something out every day. Toby saw his daughter take many things out the door; he began to save things in his room beside the bed and set up a memorial for Sue.

One day, Joe called Toby and asked, "How is the family doing?"

He answered with a lost mind, "I have not heard from your brother or your sister, I could not tell you how they are doing."

Toby did not want to go live in a retirement home. Instead, he was rebellious, and he would say, "Do whatever you want to do!"

Lake's son Junk moved out of Toby's house and went to stay with a friend.

Toby called Joe and said, "Your sister looks like your cousin who learned how to ride a horse and she is now thinking like her, she is having a good time with her girlfriend right now."

Joe and May were thinking, "Lake wants to choose that life; it is in her. Toby cannot choose her life; she is a grown woman."

Lake called once a month; Dan would get mad and he might call every two or three months, or he might not call for almost four months.

After four months, Lake came home and stayed with Toby, starting all over again. She pushed him, saying he needed to sell that house and move into a retirement home. Toby began to play with Dan and Lake; one day he might sell, and the next day he might not. He flip-flopped for almost a year and a half.

Shortly, Dan and Lake figured out how to get Toby to change his mind; they said, "If you move into retirement housing, they have lots of widows; think about all the women you can play with."

That was the attention that got Toby to change his mind; he sold his house and moved into a retirement home. For almost two years, Dan and Lake pushed Toby to change his living will. May did not have a problem with Toby going to stay in retirement housing; she thought he should.

But why push him to go there? Why did he have to change his will? They had been arguing since Sue died, and the next day Lake was pushing him; why? If he wanted to die in that house, then he should have been allowed to; it was in his will.

The next time Toby called, Joe said, "You told me you did not want to live in a retirement home. Were you forced to move into this retirement home?"

"Kind of, but not," he said; what kind of answer was he giving Joe?

Toby answered by writing a long letter to Joe. That letter said, "Yes, I have said I do not want to live in a retirement home, but your brother and Lake told me that I will be around lots of widows, and I have been thinking, soul searching, and living a fast life; it may be a good idea that I live there. And you and your brother should come here and get what you want before Lake takes all your mom's stuff out to the trash. Lake has been trashing a lot of her things."

When Joe read that letter, he got angry and said, "Soul searching? What is he thinking, he's going to find another soul mate? This is getting too masochistic for a man of that age, that fast life he has been living!"

Lake and Junk had been finding that he was not happy living at that moment; Lake was taking out her mother's things; that is stealing. She was acting like she was helping her father, but she put her mother's things in storage in her name.

Joe said, "There is nothing in that house but Lake's things; when she moved into our father's house, she rented a storage unit and took her bed and clothes, there was no room for her things. After that, she took out our mother's things, which Dad's letter said; now she is trying to take over his house."

May heard Joe's anger toward Lake and Dan. May told Joe, "Please calm down, anger is not going to solve problem."

Joe could not stop; he said, "Why is my sister filching? When she was divorcing her second husband, she had to sell her house, and he should have gotten half the money, but he did not know that she had stolen it from him. Mother told me about it; when our aunt died, Lake was taken care of in the will; she had to sell the house, and she put the things in that house into storage. They did not have children, and the will did not talk about it, but she wanted to marry another man. He had a child already, and she forged his signature. Why shouldn't I be angry at my sister? She's a thief, she is trying to take Father's house now!"

May do not know what to say to him; she just said, "Anger is not going to make you happy."

Joe said, "They have been stealing from me all my life, and they fill me with hate."

May was quiet and then thought about her mother, Kim: "Mom, I am so sorry, I was not there to help and comfort you when you needed me, please forgive me with your kind heart, I am glad that you helped me to grow into who I am, I thank you so much."

One must not forget, being a parent is not to be an unmannerly and barbarian hoodlum to one's child, like Toby was. Parents cannot, must not, should not choose one child over another. Children are not made to please their parents, parents should please their children. If a child is crying, then the parents need to stand by that child to find out what the matter is and help. Bringing a child into the world means living with hope and love, teaching them what is right and wrong, and helping them to grow.

A child did not ask to be brought into this world; we, as adults, brought them into this world.

Toby did not understand that Lake was rebellious from the childhood she had, and now it was time for her to pay him back for all her anger and pain. Lake was done being quiet, not letting anyone know how much she had been hurt.

Dan and Joe did not see Lake's pain, but May knew; May had been in her shoes once upon a time, yet May had no one to tell other than her mother, Kim. May could feel Lake's pain; she knew why she was rebelling against Toby. Yet Lake had not been nice to May; instead, she was jealous over the attention Toby paid to her. As parents, we are responsible for our child's quality of life. A child wants to be good, but Toby did not give Joe and Otto and Kay what they needed to have a good childhood. Toby was an unpleasant person. He was jealous over everything; it did not matter whether he did wrong or someone did not agree with him. Toby wanted attention and wanted women to pay attention to him whether she had a boyfriend or was married or not.

May tried to work with Joe and with Otto and Kay; she said, "It is not only you, it is all of us working together; blaming each other and crying is not going to work, and please do not bully anyone; instead, be nice; it is much better than being mean!"

Toby tried to talk to Dan about what was happening, but Dan did not care, and Joe did not care that he was alone; the only thing he wanted was an apology from Toby; he wanted his father to say, "I am so sorry that what I have done is wrong, and please forgive me."

Toby sent another e-mail to Joe, saying, "I had a phone call from the manager; there is a room available in the location I wanted; I am looking forward to moving in. I am having an open house in four days, and I would like you to come see what you think of it. And one other note, you and your brother need to come over here and take a look at everything and take what you want. Time is running out, do you care to see? Or you do not care?"

In the same e-mail, Lake wrote, "It is good, let Dan and June know that we are having an open house."

The e-mail was addressed to Dan and Joe. Joe read the e-mail; Toby was begging his two sons to go to the house and take what they wanted. Old selfish Toby did not know how to say where he was going; the begging was not working, and he was on a lonely road, going by himself. His two sons and daughter, and seven grandchildren, and two great-grandchildren did not care where he was going. The family was heartless and pitiless.

That week Dan called to set the time when he would meet with Joe and help their father. He wrote to Joe, "My neighbor is a trucker, how do I talk to those kinds of people?"

Joe asked, "Do you need anything from Sue?"

May said to Joe, "What is left? It has all been taken by your sister Lake, and I do not want anything, so please do not bring anything."

Dan called to make sure that Joe was coming to help. As he was talking, Joe got mad, and the more he spoke, the madder he got. He talked to his brother about what their father said in the letter about the neighbor who was a trucker and the price he wrote on some old china cabinet.

May thought Joe was going to blow a fuse, he was so mad that he was foaming at the mouth, and he called Dan names, saying, "He is nothing but a used car salesman."

At that moment, May had to get off the phone because she knew something was going to happen. May said to Dan, "I do not want to have that china cabinet or any other things; my children do not need to have anything from their house, please do not send any of Grandfather's things here."

Dan was begging May to take these things.

With that, the two brothers tried to take the china cabinet to the truck; Toby stopped them and said, "I think this china cabinet should go to my granddaughter, Miss Nick—. When your mother was alive she would clean for us; for that, she should have this."

The two brothers looked at each other, lost and dumfounded; they said, "What the hell is he trying to say? What is the matter with him?" The two brothers shook their heads.

As Toby was moving in, the two brothers joked, "Have you met women in this place?"

He answered, "They are all Wal-mart girls!"

Joe wondered why he thought he came from somewhere high class. He was not rich, he was a bum that liked to take from anyone he could, and he called these ladies Wal-mart girls, please.

May knew Toby had no chance. He was moving into two rooms, and he had to cook for himself. His mind was dumb.

Joe's final thought was, "I am slipping away from this family; I have no interest in what I call my father. Lake is going to stay in that house, so let her take that house; the family I thought I had was nothing but has given me uncertainty and doubt. I will not go over there to help my father and please my sister, she has put all I believe into the trash and darkened my heart. I no longed believe in this family. I only can tell my children, Otto and Kay, with my wife that I am so sorry that I have not given them a better life; I did not realize it before now. At the same time, I am feeling my wife is slipping away from me; therefore, I am trying to do what I can do to save this family."

Joe understood May's reaction, there was no longer an intimate feeling between husband and wife. Joe said to May, "I feel you are slipping away from me."

May had to tell him the truth; she called him and said, "You have been my best friend before, and now, I have no place to go and neither do you, for right now our friendship survives and we are business partners; we live for now, not know what the future holds."

CHAPTER 31
Out and Out Infamous for Good

All journeys have a secret that many travelers are unaware of. May married to cherish a thought, but it was broken with a phantom, frivolous head. It was long hard work, she remembered the children's birthdays but never their age. She remembered the good and bad times, simplicity is the peak of civilization, and everyday life was a special occasion that May wanted to lead on. May thought she was on the right track, but life always gets harder the closer you get to the summit, even though she did not sit and wait.

May thought, "If I do not have time to live now, then when will I have time?"

Voting in the election was an anticlimax, after the two-faced e-mail, it took the polar opposite in character; you did not know who you thought you knew before and now you ask, "Which person are you?"

There was no answer, instead, they would say, "I have a friend who is black and from another country."

The excuse was a galvanizing lie, gaiety with the gaggle.

May still receives harassing e-mails from the family; she said, "Do

I care about Internet bullies? I do not; I have done my job, which could help change this country. I did it with my heart and with my honor; if they have a problem, then it is their problem." May added, "They say they have friends who are different colors; then why do they have a problem with Muslims?"

May wanted to trust Dan. After she voted in the election, Dan showed he was unmannerly and boorish. You might say it is a hard world, but you must think back to May; she has spent thirty-five years in hardship and a miserable life. May tried to forgive the family and integrate them into positive intellect. The election gave May a voice to speak. One more thing, when she went into the voting booth, it was a skirmish, and people were mocking and scornful. But May did not back off; her feet were firm, and she walked into the voting room and spoke with her voice in the voting booth. When she went out, her pride was high and her spirit felt better than if she had taken cocaine.

When your self-worth goes up, then your net worth goes up with it. May tried hard in many ways. She tried to bring up her self-esteem; Lake was intrusive and meddlesome. Clearly, Lake had lived a lie for years. She asked May for help with math problems when Cary was trying to become a nurse, yet Lake forgot that and mocked May, demeaning her with a verbal attack to humiliate and embarrass her in front of all the cousins.

Does this mean Lake is smart? No; she made herself look like a stupid, feebleminded, simple person.

May did not argue with Lake; instead, she let her talk all she wanted and showed herself to be a loser. We can point to a child as being a bully, but May said that was no way to treat a child; she said, "I am not going to be that hateful person; a child sees, and then a child does, like Toby showed the family he was a bully— revolting, loathsome, and repugnant. Lake learned from Toby and she became like Toby. We should always blame the parents if a child is a bully; we should look into where the child learned it from. As adults, we can learn from our mistakes and try to be good parents, but some parents cannot; they are narcissistic and use their children for a capital gain. I do not think Lake will be a grown woman. Overall, the family inherited Toby's narcissism and jealousy."

May tried to cleanse her mind and have a good laugh and a good cry; many times she failed to stand on her two feet. She promised her children that she loved them more than anything. May laughed with them and cried with them. When she laughed with her children, it brought May joy to see what Otto and Kay became. When she cried, she always had a hope to look for. And she always saw the children's future; she had sad and happy moments, tears of joy and cleansing laughter.

May did not train as a worker. She did not know where to go to get her fortune. She believed in hope and doing things honestly to get a fortune. There were many years of the cold shoulder from the frightful, ugly, disgusting, horrifying, atrocious family May married into.

May did not give up; she promised her children, "I will not leave you, and I will always be there when you need it."

May did not grow up with her birth father. She promised her children, "You will have your birth father there when you need it."

Looking back, May had a good life with her stepfather, but at a young age, she rebelled against her mother; she did not get enough attention from her mother and thought her birth father would be better. She said, "Now I am grown and have learned that it does not matter, birth father or stepfather notwithstanding, yet nevertheless Toby should not and must not be around children; he is not a good father or grandfather to any children."

Good fortune is what happens before and now; one should give children trust and a place to sleep without harm and with a warm blanket on the bed so they can dream. Too many wounds, it takes time to heal, and the chapter needs to be closed. Whether you have been hurt or happy, yesterday is history. There is no need to be sad or cry; the only thing to do is learn from one's mistakes and look to the future.

May said to the family, "Why do we argue and hurt each other? Where else can I go to have peace of mind? I would like to share this with you: I am not greedy or hurtful to others. If you want to know me, then I have a moment of hope and care. But please do not go after my children; if you have any questions, I can answer what you want to hear."

Finally, a loser does not have good action, does not matter, and doesn't have a mind of care and hope; losers act by bullying and displaying jealousy, greed, and racial discrimination. "I must act as always in good matters to any others." This family had been frivolous and showed a failure to yield.

May's last thought: "I thought that coming to America meant everything was going to be rich and glamorous. But it was a whirlwind passing by; let the dust off it. Use it, and enjoy it after a long period of neglect. I did not know about the dirty little secret hidden under the rug. No doubt, I have been neglected by this harsh environment. But I chose to be in this world, and I cannot blame it. Evil does teach us bad and good, and if there is no evil, there is no angel. The biggest elephant is scared of the littlest mouse, smaller than his toe. So does it matter whether it is big or small? All parts of the continent have history. We live with history. No one can give you what you need; you must believe with honesty and creativity. Love is not taken; love should be given to a child. What your friend tells you about the other person hides failure with intentionally false statements. Moreover, I must dominate my belief in government. Giving up is failure. I will not give up forever and ever."

Getting to know May's story was eye-opening. May has lived in this country almost thirty-six years; she voted in seven presidential elections. It took courage and guts, and she took a journey with her children without help; it was a dangerous, risky journey. May did not know with her first and second child; she imagined she wanted to be a good mother and promised her children. When she stepped off the plane, she was a bony ninety-five-pound girl who spoke no English and had no job. She thought she would meet Indian scalpers and she would help unchain the slaves' ankles. She was married to a blue-eyed husband, yet she lived an organic life as well as she could. After all the criticism from his gutless family, she is standing firm and living with hope.

Author Biography

Mi. Odle came from South Korea. She came to this country with hope and belief that her dream could come true. But she did not see or experience the glamorous life that she read about. But with her education from South Korea high school before she came to this country, and the lesson her mother gave her that a glamorous life is not given, a glamorous life is given with yourself, as you have to work it out.